LUMINOUS CITIES

EDUARDO GARCÍA AGUILAR

TRANSLATED BY JAY MISKOWIEC

ILLUSTRATED BY SANTIAGO REBOLLEDO

ALIFORM PUBLISHING
MINNEAPOLIS

ALIFORM PUBLISHING
is part of The Aliform Group
117 Warwick Street /Minneapolis, MN USA 55414
information@aliformgroup.com www.aliformgroup.com

Originally published in Spanish as *Urbes Luminosas*
© Leega, 1991

First published in the United States of America by
Aliform Publishing, 2002

Copyright © Eduardo García Aguilar, 1991
English translation copyright © Aliform Publishing, 2002

Library of Congress Control Number
2002107838

ISBN 0-9707652-1-5

Printed in the United States of America
Set in Times New Roman
Cover art by Santiago Rebolledo
Cover design by Carolyn M. Fox

First Edition of the English Translation

LUMINOUS CITIES

ALSO BY EDUARDO GARCÍA AGUILAR

ESSAY
Celebraciones y otros fantasmas: una biografía
    intelectual de Álvaro Mutis
Delirio de San Cristóbal: Manifiesto para una
    generación desencantada
(English translation: Mexico Madness: Manifesto
    for a Disenchanted Generation)
García Márquez: la tentación cinematográfica

NARRATIVE
Bulevar de los héroes
(English translation: Boulevard of Heroes)
Cuaderno de sueños
Palpar la zona prohibida
Tierra de leones
Urbes luminosas
El viaje triunfal

POETRY
Ciudades imaginarias
Llanto de la espada

CONTENTS

LUMINOUS CITIES

I. ORGIES AND MANNEQUINS

II. GARRETS AT THE END OF THE WORLD

III. STENDHAL AND FLAUBERT IN THE STOMACH

List of Illustrations

Translator's Introduction

      This illustrated translation came together like a scene from one of the tales told in this book: not long after the turn of the millennium an American writer sits at a bar drinking mezcal late one night in the luminous city of Oaxaca. The man strikes up a conversation with the stranger beside him, a painter from Colombia who has lived in Mexico half his life. They talk about this magical region in which they find themselves, then about the art and literature of the Americas; they praise some of the same films, dislike some of the same artists, and have read some of the same books, including *Urbes luminosas,* short stories by a Colombian writer living in Paris, who as the muses would have it happens to be a friend of them both.

      The painter begins sculpting his vision of these cities, and the translator describes how these places change and stay the same as they are transposed from one language to another. By the time the two emerge into the dawn beneath the shadow of Monte Albán, they have inexorably become protagonists in an endeavor of languages and images that always already awaited them in some literary world.

The characters in Eduardo García Aguilar's short stories and novels are often exiles, wanderers, foreigners, and that is because he has never ceased what he calls the eternal circumnavigation to which his compatriots are destined. The cities he explores and describes in the following texts—sometimes like an archeologist, sometimes like a stranger lost in a strange land—are seen from the inside out: not their monuments or landmarks, but their skylines and streets spied from garret windows, their sewers and subway tunnels and warehouses haunted by abandoned solitary beings.

These tales are set amidst events like earthquakes, political assassinations and funerals, but they are also peopled with lovers finding each other for the first time, friends watching the sunset, poor men enjoying a simple meal in the restaurant of an unknown neighborhood: fleeting moments of time in places half-drawn, the barely glimpsed experiences of people we just brush past, like in real life.

García Aguilar celebrates the city itself. Paris and Mexico City reign here, the two places that have most formed and informed the author's work and life over the last twenty years: the worlds of Flaubert and Huysmans and Sartre, Cuauhtémoc and Nervo and Paz: the capital of Europe seen through the eyes of a Latin American; the biggest, greatest urb of the New World that resuscitates in the foreign visitor millenarian visions and indescribable pleasures as the author has described in so many places factual and fictive.

As a journalist—a profession he has criticized for imposing a sort of false objectivity and distancing on the writer—García Aguilar covered civil conflicts and revolutions in Central America, witnessing what has so succinctly been called man's inhumanity to man. Those experiences also come forth here in stories that lead to abrupt, shocking endings, as the world of war often does. For the heirs of magic realism who have grown up amidst dictatorships and *narcos* and an all too prevalent global mass media, there is nothing more mystical or terrifying than the actual, concrete world which rules over our lives.

Luminous Cities is a cosmic map drawn by a delirious cartographer, the picaresque diary of a professional foreigner: "dreams like a white silk curtain."

JM, City of Lakes, 2002

True memories seemed like phantoms, while false memories were so convincing that they replaced reality.
Gabriel García Márquez, *Strange Pilgrims*

I am an intruder here. I am an intruder in a world unaccustomed to intrusion. A world separate from the world...
Carlos Fuentes, *Terra Nostra*

That may have been the one hour ever to enhance the street with a spell, giving it privileges of tenderness, making it real like a legend or verse: what is certain is that I felt it remotely near, like a memory which arrives exhausted only because it comes from the depths of the soul.
Jorge Luis Borges, "Unknown Street"

LUMINOUS CITIES

I

ORGIES AND MANNEQUINS

Tjüren Ferdinand

FOR HALF A YEAR I worked as a dishwasher at Tjüren Ferdinand, a restaurant on the outskirts of Stockholm. To get there from the university housing in Freskati I would take a bus coming exactly at 6:08 a.m., as the schedules stuck on the station walls announced, that later passed down a highway bordered by flowers. On the road stood Carolinska Hospital and a vivarium of exotic plants. At the bus terminal young women dressed like cowgirls skated around an ice rink and more than one drunk sprawled on the grounds of the luxurious homes in Taby. The restaurant was located in a large commercial center where residents from the north side of Stockholm gathered, its doors reached by a long set of escalators. The owner of the place was an Egyptian with a thick black moustache who had lived in Sweden for twenty years. None of his children looked like they came from the banks of the Nile.

In the Tjüren Ferdinand worked the boyfriends of his daughters and the girlfriends of his sons, the picture completed by a couple of old Turks, a pair of Yugoslavians, two young Polish women and a young Colombian. The Yugoslavians looked like they were out of an old John Travolta movie and they would threaten the other foreigners with huge cleavers they used to chop meat. The Poles would splash on entire bottles of French perfume, and while the detritus spattered against the walls amid the viscous bustle of their work, they reeked of Chanel and Helena Rubinstein. The old Turks, both of them plump and pompous, appeared like characters from some Asian film. The solidarity and tenderness they held for their young coworkers was astonishing.

In the mornings before work began we would all play the roulette slot machines, sometimes winning as much or more than we received in salary. By the end of our shifts we employees became each other's understanding brother, having drunk over the course of the day an entire keg of beer. At night after work we would go party hard at long summertime fiestas, places that dazzled with the beauty of drunk girls sprawling next to trees or beneath the stages where bands played songs by Elvis Presley. The Yugoslavians made jokes about Tito and the Poles told stories about Gierek while, possessed by the deliciousness of capitalism, they bathed themselves with flasks of cologne and smeared themselves with shampoo and vodka.

One day after a scuffle the older Yugoslavian threatened me with a kitchen knife and I, having drunk quite a few beers, challenged him to fight in front of the Polish girls. The man finally put down his knife, but not until he'd grazed my stomach with the fateful blade. After that the idyllic atmosphere was broken,

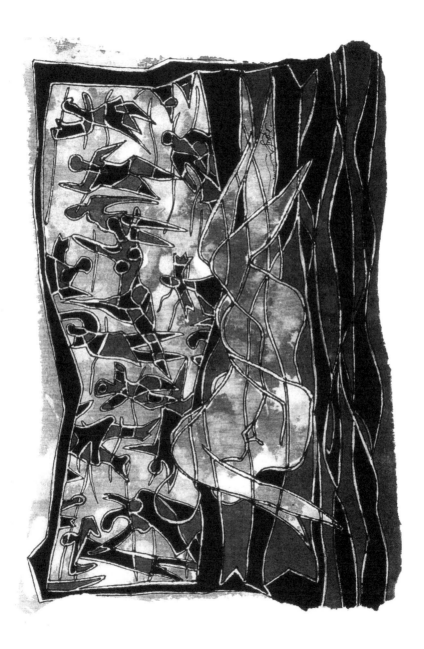

but I had won the love of the two sylphs from Warsaw. One was short and fat, the other a thin sociology student who had read Marcuse and Foucault. We all let the petty cook play the ridiculous role of the failed chef, dressed in his tall hat and long white apron. Admiring my valor, the Polish sociologist said nothing was possible in Poland and then threw herself at me, covering me with kisses. Later in a warehouse full of bald and naked mannequins, we entwined ourselves in an afternoon of love, interrupted only by the distance whistle of the train heading back to Stockholm.

We went to the mannequin depot everyday. They were every size and color and their eyes shone with an intensive neon light. In one corner about a thousand wigs were piled together. One day we saw something moving amid the sinister hides of hair. The Pole approached it and picked up a bust standing next to the door. Out of the disorder emerged the head of a little blue-eyed man with messy hair who stunk beyond words. He had a weak chin and thin lips that displayed either happiness or cynicism. We offered him a drink, and as he stumbled over to join us, we could see his pockets were full of books. Sitting on the butt of a female mannequin, the man recounted to us how for some time he had worked as the guardian of those figures we saw cast about everywhere throughout the warehouse, but that his true vocation was that of novelist. "With what I earn in four months," he said, "I can go write for an entire year in Paris. But," he added, "I end up spending everything the first day and then just living on air."

The man said his name was Joseph Roth and he was the author of *The March of Radetsky, Job, Confession of a Killer,* and *The Legend of the Holy Drinker.*

"But you died in 1939," the naked Polish sociologist said to him in an astonished voice, leafing through the books the man passed to her with trembling hands.

"Forgive me," he replied, "it's that sometimes I lose track of time. You know, cognac does its damage. The novel and cognac will end up driving anybody crazy. Novelists lose sight of reality and confuse their characters with real beings, and vice versa. Time gets turned upside down. It takes such great effort to create another world within this world that the invented devours the real, as fiction sponges off the person who produces it. Well, why don't we have a drink..."

He took a bottle from his pocket and passed it around. "You are the Pole, and," he said, turning to me, "You are the Colombian. I was born in Russian Galicia and died desperate in Paris. My last book was *The Legend of the Holy Drinker*. They published it posthumously and my friend Hermann Kesten wrote an account of my last days..."

Roth tumbled backwards over the wigs and fell asleep just as he had been when we found him. He snored and his smooth white hands fidgeted against his black overcoat. We dressed and began to walk past the ten-thousand mannequins. A strange noise of plaster resounded in the enormous enclosure and then we saw them blink their eyes and stand up. They lined up beside the door and one after the other began to leave. Roth went on sleeping. We let them go and then observed the highway full of mannequins. We took the train and there saw nothing but bald figures with blank gazes. That night the mannequins took possession of the city and named one of their own winner of the Nobel Prize.

The Delirium of San Felipe Neri

THE OLD WALLS of the baroque church are covered with wounds, holes provoked by gunfights from other eras. Around the scars concentrate lichens and moss that survive nourished by the rain. The golden altars inside, interwoven with delirious images of martyred saints and the warm faces of angels, shine with a dry light slightly obscured by the smoke of incense and the sweat of a thousand faithful. Enormous floral arrangements in showy, tawdry colors impregnate the mystical midday atmosphere with their somber smell. Organ music surges from a secret place while women cross themselves and lower their veiled, hidden faces.

In the middle of the ceremony some young people dressed in black jackets enter by one of the doors and head toward the empty altar. There they take out their instruments and begin playing heavy metal rock, twisting and turning, jumping over the kneelers and lancing insults at the faithful and the priests who throw themselves upon the sacrilegious youth, beating them with censers and burning candles.

From a large carriage parked before the atrium descends a group of eighteenth-century libertines, their long powdered wigs and clothing absurd in the oppressive heat and the epoch in which these events occur. They spread out among the faithful, unsheathe long whips and climb atop the altar to teach the black-coated rockers a lesson. The latter are tied to the columns with chains that the priests and nuns quite quickly portion out, calming the public. In the pulpit a French filmmaker hastily films the scene, while another priest dressed in purple delivers a sermon and waves his arms in terror, as if blinded by the divine forces of guilt.

The rockers' instruments lay sprawled about the floor. Someone has trampled the electric guitars and the bass has been thrown down upon the steps and sprinkled with holy water. The oldest libertine spies the group's female singer and takes off her jacket. In the light her body remains covered by leather clothes and calfskin boots. He lashes her with the whip for several minutes. The tall woman still seems happy and demands that the libertine, whose mature age is recognized in the wrinkles in his face and the dark circles around his eyes, whip her even harder. Then he licks her bloody body. Several nuns interrupt him and lash him in turn: as they undress him they discover he is a priest and hang him with his chasuble next to the painting of the Virgin of Sorrows. The organist goes wild playing an extraordinary music which makes the cupolas vibrate and breaks the keystones of the central arches. A beautiful nun shows her breasts to the astonished multitude who raise their supplications to heaven and cross themselves, coughing from the insupportable smoke of the censor that mixes with the scorching of the burning body: the nuns have set on fire the libertine or priest under order of the beautiful bloody rocker, until all that remains are ashes. The bassist starts a solo and slowly his companions begin to accompany him, the organist joining this delirious symphony never before heard by mortals.

The noise is so great the ceramic angels loosen from the walls and altars and crash onto the hard floor. People have calmed down and continue praying in the vast nave of the baroque temple. Everyone concentrates on the magisterial concert. Suddenly the nun who showed off her breasts from the organist's niche climbs up to the pulpit and begins singing with the aid of the microphone. First she takes off her cowl and then begins to slowly take off her clothes in front of the meek and faithful, who place their floral arrangements next to the confessionals. The nun is of an unequalled allure. Seeing her naked, no one can avoid the feeling of encountering beauty personified in that mysterious woman. No one with all their senses intact can avoid converting to her religion, to her rites, to being her follower for centuries to come. "Amen! Amen!" is heard throughout the enclosure. A beggar without feet or hands or eyes or tongue crawls from the atrium and passes down the church's center aisle, creeping along like some strange beast described by an insomniac traveler or drug addict. "Amen! Amen!" screams the creature, whose nauseating smell is overwhelming. He approaches the rock group and standing up he dances, twisting and contorting his miserable, frightening little body. He laughs. He opens his mouth and emits moans and alleluiahs. The nun descends from the pulpit and goes to calm him down. The man cries and she dries his tears, caressing his dirty hair, his indescribable face. The singer also climbs down to the place where the creature creeps along to caress and sooth him.

Several of the faithful arrive with a beautiful golden conveyance on their shoulders—a carriage that in other times would have served to receive viceroys and archbishops, abbots and priests—and place the monster in it. Calm is finally restored and everyone acclaims him the true messiah, raising their hands and praying for his eternal glory. The uproar increases in the street and next to the doors of the church crowd together the inhabitants of the city. The rock singer and the nun are his ladies-in-waiting and they climb into the carriage that several strong men bear with happiness and pride. The procession passes through the city, lashed now by a lightening storm. Behind the cortege follow the rockers playing heavy metal music alongside the priests who waft incense and sprinkle holy water. The monster belches and laughs, gazed upon by his two beautiful, irresistible tutors.

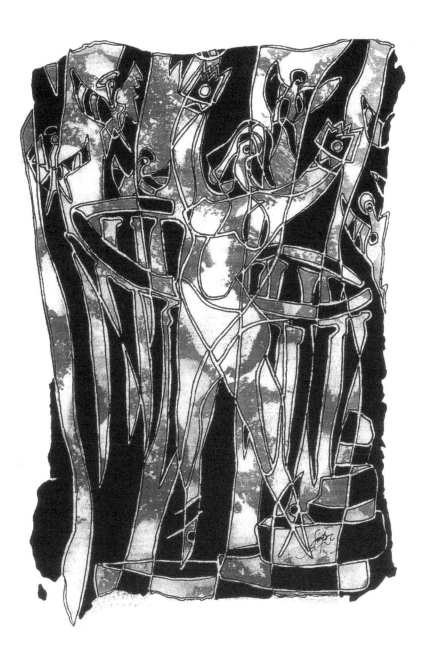

The Grand Show of Panama

FROM THE HOTEL COLÓN, an old edifice with vast, cool rooms, a line of ships can be seen in the distance awaiting authorization to enter the Panama Canal. At night there are gleams of light that sprinkle over the sea, intense unfurling colors, titillating stains of light. The heat is suffocating, but the breeze calms a bit the daytime stupor. The streets are full of garbage and rotting fruit rinds. Downtown the traces of the agitated day are found in the doors of whorehouses where beautiful women from Central and South America dance on a tiny red-carpeted stage. One of them, extraordinarily beautiful, far more than any national or provincial beauty queen, begins a surprising striptease before the agitated crowd, bringing out of their cubbyholes rheumatic old men who blow their noses, foolish beings with alcoholic faces who dribble on the tables filled with rum and cokes and glasses of whiskey. She disappears behind the curtain and a fat woman daubed with sparkle comes out and dances to a sordid old melody of Luisito Rey. The woman strips immodestly in front of the drunken audience, showing them her enormous cellulite-covered thighs, her grotesque white tits, a formless, almost gelatinous hanging mass. There are still those who applaud and throw themselves at her when she finishes her doleful show. Then a fourteen-year-old girl appears. She's dressed like an adolescent rock star and her lips are painted red. She starts to undress before the crowd, displaying her slender thighs and little body that at times looks like that of a boy, just as her small breasts seem like simple pre-pubescent teats. Through a small door comes another girl in a blue cap who begins to dance around the beautiful youth, first taking her white flannel top off and then her panties, finally concluding with an agitated copulation that drives the spectators crazy. Later after they've gone offstage come a few clowns that tell jokes until a man with a shaved skull and gallows air, wearing a black leather jacket, enters and begins beating them until they're bloody. The red clown noses, the powdered white wigs, the little shoes with long tongues, the brightly hued jackets and the pants with garishly colored flowers scatter over the stage as the audience applauds.

Waiters come and go with their precious cargo. In the middle of the performance a man shoots someone and immediately the forces of order take charge of removing the wounded and the aggressor. But still everything calmly goes on. Intermission lasts almost an hour. Tropical music plays over the speakers and a few couples go out and dance on the tiny dance floor. The strippers dance with the men, most of them foreigners ready now after a long voyage to squander their money on a night of pleasure. Among those in attendance are soldiers, Bolivian merchants, Finnish sailors, captains from Senegal and Haiti, salesmen from multinational companies, buyers of cheap products and gifts and worthless trinkets they will take back to Nicaragua or Honduras.

The show resumes. They've already taken away the props of the beaten clowns and now present two handicapped people fucking. This is the main show tonight, because besides being in wheelchairs they are both deaf and mute and their gestures, their movements performed to the sound of an extraordinary music enflame with passion the respectable drunks, to whom nothing now seems strange. In the end everyone in the bar is crawling on the floor when suddenly the curtain comes down to make way for a transvestite act. There are three of them, dressed like the caricatures of women with the neutered beauty of vamps. Heavy metal rock plays and the transvestites mimic the singers of slovenly bands that recall the Dead Kennedys or Sigmund Freud. Someone murmurs they're foreigners from Venezuela and their act was a hit in Miami. The music ends at three in the morning.

Outside on the street you feel a breeze dragging along more garbage and more rotting matter. On a long street with the sweaty odor of daytime bodies, the wind beats against the white walls and blue shutters while beggars sleep on the sidewalks next to supermarkets or little food stands open late. A sizzling music is heard in the distance. Three blocks farther on in an empty lot an orchestra enlivens an outdoor festival. Women and men, little children and teenagers, gray-haired old men and toothless old ladies dance to a music that sounds like calypso mixed with a few

Creole tones. They dance furiously, unendingly, and nobody who passes by can avoid joining in and mixing with the crazed mass that has lost the notion of time and the feeling in their bodies. They create an incessant wave, injected with the narcotic of dancing. One can greet dawn like this, not stopping for an instant, covered with sweat, eyes closed, desiring the bodies of the women wandering through the dancers. Pairs possessed by a kiss stand beneath lamp posts, men cover the chosen women with their hands like octopi and press them against the wooden walls of beer and whiskey warehouses. Survivors of the show will one after the other fall puking at the edge of the dance floor, while pickpockets rob their wallets and at times strike them in the face. The blood of a few victims mixes with the puddles left behind by the afternoon rain. Morning arrives and the sun begins beating down. Later, after the cumbia players and the calypso dancers have gone off, you see the pale violated tourists, dead as rag dolls. In their stands the beer vendors make love on old straw mattresses and the sound coming through the wooden walls can be discerned in the morning silence. Once again a musky sweat invades the air circulating through the streets that begin filling with people. In the distance the ships awaiting authorization to enter the canal doze in the tropical waters, strange floating animals whose silhouettes tremble in the surging waves.

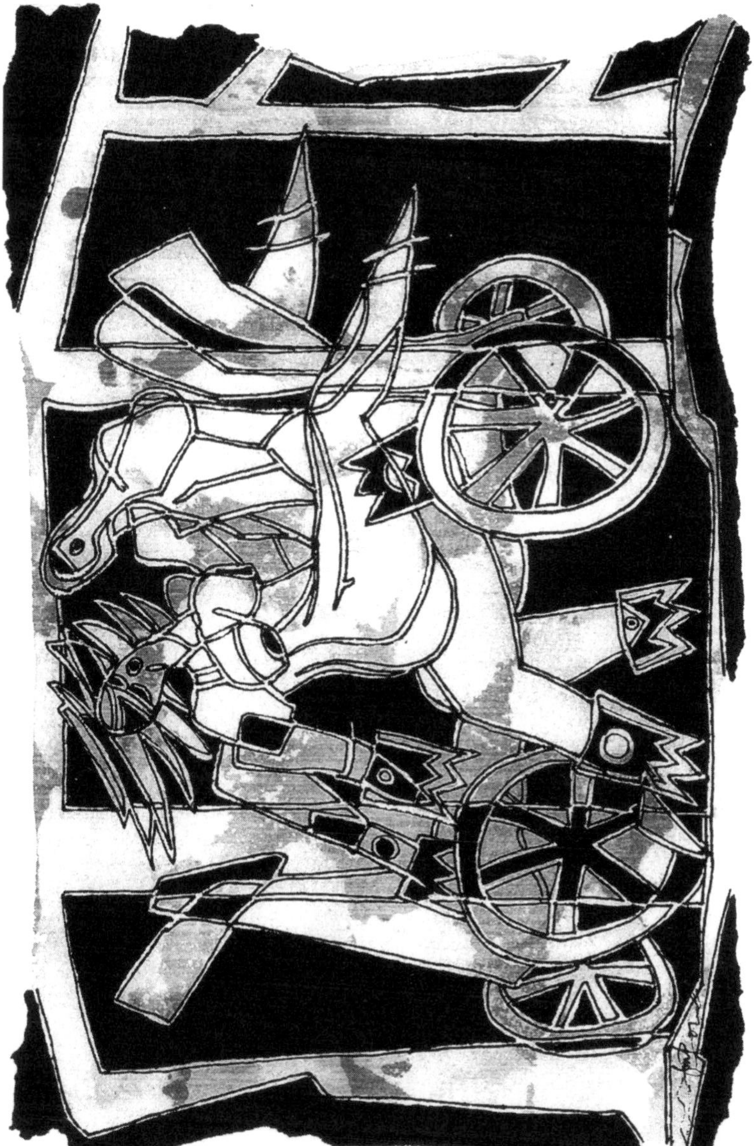

Passion Flower

BY THE TIME he arrived to Rome afternoon was ending. The smell of espresso floated over the platforms of the train station while the crowd coming from abroad and other parts of the country hurriedly went out into the streets. He boarded a green double-decker bus and let himself be carried off without much of an idea where it was going. A secret feeling guided him toward the center of the city where he would spend the night. He had made a long two-day journey from Paris and the motive behind his flight was amorous indignation: his lover, a young girl whose pussy drove men crazy, had abandoned him, leaving him submerged in a profound sadness. Still, some woman accompanied him to the train station to say goodbye after having consoled him for several days.

The trip was really an accident. In the first car he traveled in company of a group of Red Brigade sympathizers, lulled to sleep by the conversation of that cell of young anarchists making plans to destroy cathedrals, train terminals, old buildings and patriotic monuments. It was frightfully cold and snow fell endlessly over the European countryside. At the Swiss border the train had to stop for two hours, due to a thick blanket of snow covering the rails. When the train left again at dawn, the engineers forgot the caboose, which had to wait three more hours for another train to pull it. Later they arrived to Turin and he thought of Cesare Pavese. There he changed trains. The new one was old and wooden, the compartments guarding a soft nostalgic aroma. With him went a novice, an old nun and a village priest who bombarded him with questions about his distant country and the remote customs of its inhabitants. They invited him to stay in a rectory in Rome and even proposed he enroll in the ranks of the church, an offer he immediately declined.

Now it's night and he walks through unknown streets. The date is the sixth of January. In bars that serve white wine drawn from huge wooden barrels, young people gesture with their hands while they loudly converse. He has no friends and doesn't speak Italian, but he keeps hoping to encounter someone he knows. There in the back of the bar move the faces of many young people, but nobody looks familiar. He leaves and heads to another bar, wandering for several hours about the Piazza Navona. Accosted by the cold he decides to pass through an entranceway, first opening an enormous wooden door. Inside in the darkness, he lets himself be drawn toward the warmth and decides to sleep there a bit, not having slept for several days. He dreams of an imaginary city. He has arrived on a flying carpet, accompanied by a beautiful long-haired woman dressed in an Indian sari. He enters the blue and red vegetation, dense and torrid like a jungle, and rising above it are jasper cupolas and obsidian buildings whose gleaming reflections blind and kill birds. The carpet flies over the city and begins slowly descending toward a patio where offerings of copal and incense smolder. It's quite hot. On the carpet, placed in the middle of the vast plaza, he feels the caresses of the beautiful girl who disrobes for him in the terrifying solitude of that dream world. She has a perfect body, especially round, firm breasts he kisses all afternoon. Just as they are about to make love, he is wakened by a tumult of people.

At that hour the inhabitants of the abandoned mansion arrive home drunk, possessed by the smoke of hashish. They number about ten and sing songs and dance in the patio holding bottles of liquor in their hands. When they see him lying there next to the heating duct, they gather and pick him up between them, carrying him to the third floor and a vast drawing room with wooden floors and exposed beams. There they start a party in his honor. They ask him neither his name nor nationality.

For him are the best joints of marihuana, the most exquisite sips of absinthe, the longest kisses from the night's sweetest lips. A circle of dancers forms around him and the shadows of their bodies project over the high white walls in the titillating light of aromatic candles. An incipient Indian melody mixes with the aroma of passion flower and the nocturnal sweat of the divas who move for him. He decides to wash the women's feet with a bottle of sparkling cider and he drinks the drops that fall from their toes, the spectators applauding.

Hours have passed. One by one all the women

have been his. Worn out, he sleeps and snores naked on a cushion. The light of a purple sun projects over the distant horizon. A soft thread settles over the vegetation of the imaginary city. In the distance, a few bell towers ring the morning carillon. Carnivorous green and blue flowers open their multicolored fauces. Morning explodes in a vegetal symphony. He awakes to discover he is in the plaza of his dream. He rubs his eyes. With his hands he grabs fistfuls of golden sand. He is naked and looks around, not knowing what to do or where to go. A ductile liana traps his left foot, while another wraps itself around his waist. He tries to escape, but a thin reed bends and grabs his neck. He is slowly dragged toward the jungle. A violet flower spreads its petals and as its fauces open a viscous liquid flows forth whose musk smells like passion flower. Unable to move, his eyes imploring and his mouth covered by an unmovable leaf, his skin slashed and covered by sweat, he hears the plant shriek as it begins to savor his exquisite flesh. An intense, unequalled pleasure takes hold of him and in absolute ecstasy he is sucked into the secret concavities of the carnivorous plant. His friends in Paris think he has stayed to live forever in Rome.

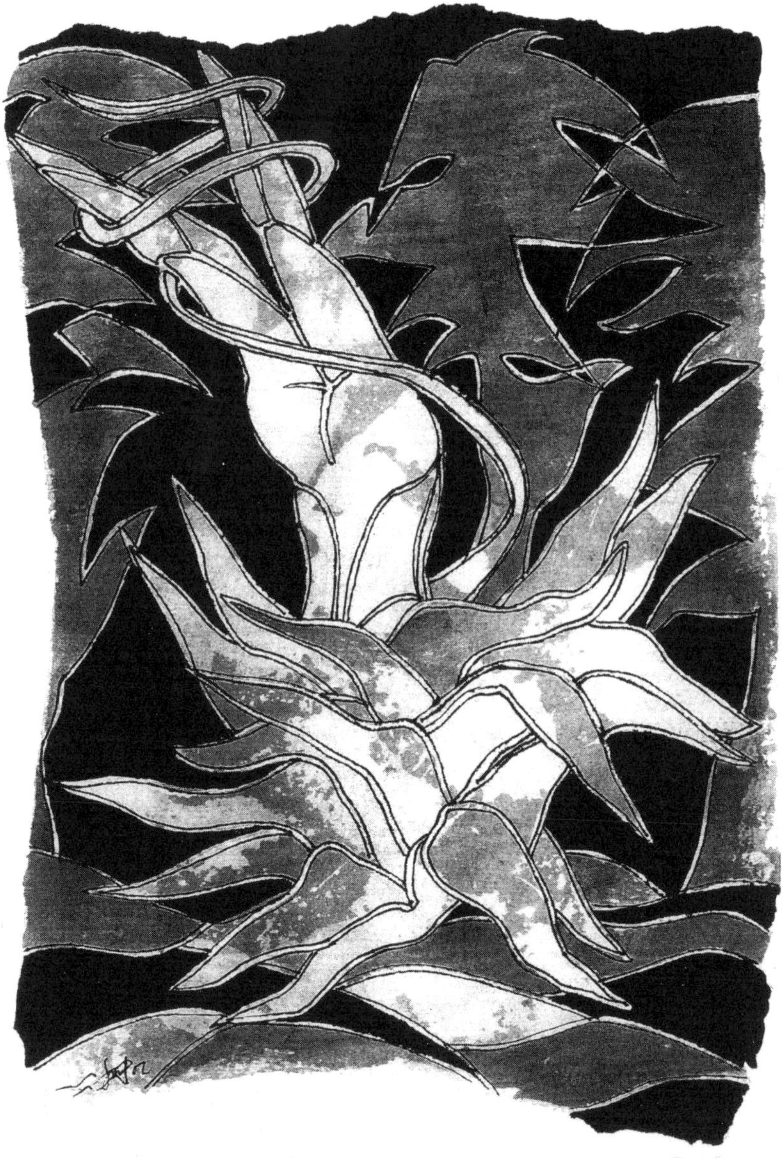

The Eunuch Ward

SOMETIMES the best places to read are hospitals. One finds there a strange antiseptic atmosphere of methylene blue that resuscitates the unlimited whiteness of the mind and facilitates concentration. The sick, sometimes strange characters anointed with phosphorescent-colored ointments lie moaning in their beds, the neon lights covering them with a patina of divine compassion. To read in the waiting room's big armchairs, the smell of medications and mentholated rubs mixing with the lively scalpels, is a pleasure few know how to accept with peace and tranquility. Once in a hospital where I was reclused by the doctors for some strange incomprehensible illness, a friend of mine lent me Rousseau's *Confessions* and Faulkner's *Light in August.*

One afternoon, as I remained alone after visiting hours and the orderlies organized the day's final tasks, I opened Jean-Jacques's book and immersed myself completely in it. That evening, after the lights had been turned off in all the wards, I managed to escape to an illuminated corridor where I could ponder how Rousseau, beyond being a great writer and precursor of the modern narrative, was also a sick man eaten away by the virus of literature. I couldn't stop, only pausing when they brought me a meal or gave me an injection, or when the nurse covered me with her strange ointments. A few scenes were so erotic that it wasn't long before I began to desire the nurse, Sylvie Krouma, a kind of slender goddess with small hands and the face of a madonna.

When they turned out the lights, Krouma, sensitive to my desperation, became my accomplice and would take me to a cubicle where she watched me read, wrapped up in the bluish bathrobe they put on all us sick people. She used to offer me tea and delicious snacks prohibited at those nocturnal hours and moreover, when I was stalked by the passionate descriptions of Rousseau, I would fall onto the couch of a recently deceased psychoanalyst and she would lean over and start undressing me with an indescribable tenderness.

Later we would make love for long hours until day broke and the doctors and nurses arrived for their daily shifts. Her face could have come out of a Renaissance painting, but her body and her long tawny legs would move upon the couch with a delicious cadence that made me moan and scream the name of Rousseau while she hurriedly covered my mouth. Since then I haven't been able to forget Jean-Jacques and not one of his celebrated scenes has been erased from my memory, despite the years.

Krouma helped me to read Faulkner. By the following week I had fallen into the clutches of the

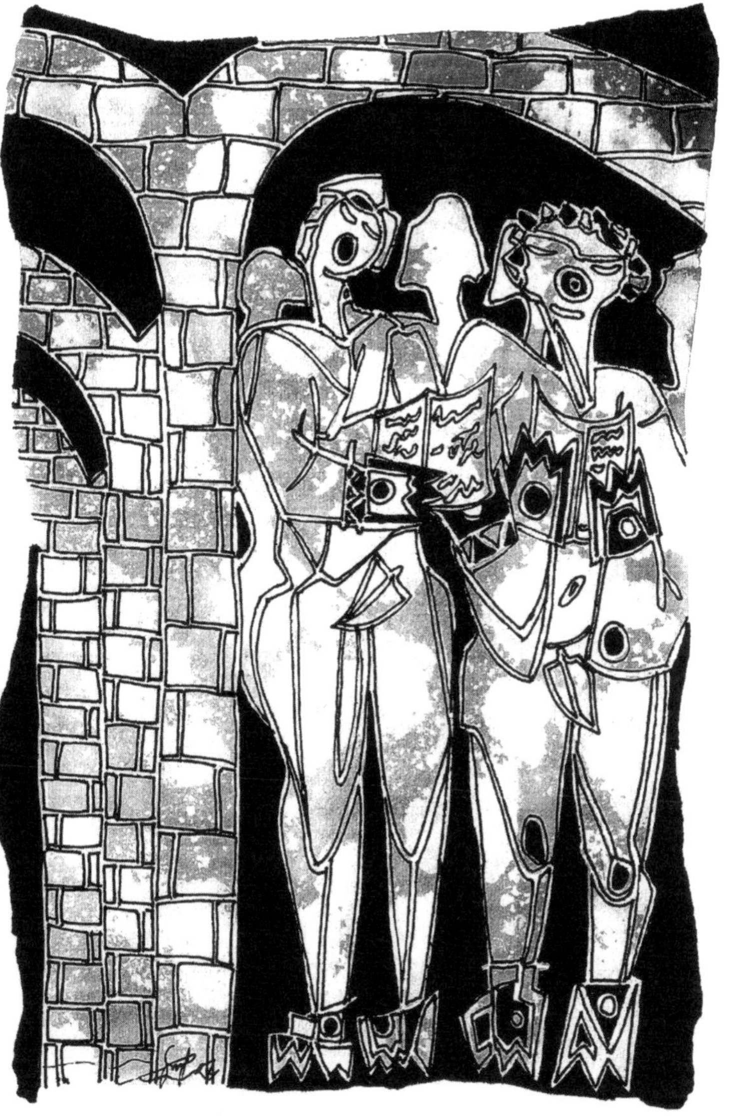

great narrator from Oxford, Mississippi. But his reading was marked by misfortune. One morning they discovered Sylvie making love with a Cambodian who used to read sacred texts and every day knelt and prayed to an unknown god. It was all so shameful that they didn't give her a chance to defend herself. Moreover, the Cambodian, who suffered from a strange illness, was expelled and sent to a terrible hospital where it seemed no one got out alive.

I can't forget the poor man's cries when several strong, brawny orderlies forced him into a gray van from which he never returned. It seemed that having lived so long in that hospital waiting to be cured of his malady he well knew the horrors awaiting him at the other hospital, and from his cries, his gaping mouth, his eyes bulging from their sockets, it was clear he had turned into a most exact metaphor of pain. When I came to the part in *Light in August* where the black man is cut down by bullets, I remembered the poor Cambodian and ever since I haven't been able to separate this man from the author of *Wild Palms*. That night I observed the empty bed of Mguyen and cried when I saw the abandoned carpet on which he would pray in his incomprehensible language. His gold-toothed smiling face and oriental friendliness passed before me each night, and the same for his cries that communicated to all the patients a terrible feeling of impotence.

Two days later a new nurse arrived, a former Vietnamese nun, they said, with lascivious lips and a tight sensual body. I had finished the books my friend gave me and had to content myself with reading a gorgeous illustrated Bible. Out of a Jacobean prurience I had never approached the sacred text until the beautiful Vietnamese woman placed it on my night stand. I got her to open the cubicle for me and there on the couch of the dead psychoanalyst I read about unforgettable adventures, not able to close my eyes for days that passed in rapid mystery. The Vietnamese woman would pass through the corridors and come into the cubicle to drink coffee and read, observing me with distance and disdain.

At three in the morning, the diminutive woman would take off her white uniform and hat and in a corner change into her tight jeans and sheer blouse. There occurred so much coupling in the Bible and so many erotic, luxurious scenes that desire wasn't long in stirring and one day I managed to seduce her, using my most subtle and secret techniques.

That woman was like a cat, agile and with an uncommon capacity for intrigue. The Bible fell to the floor, breaking a bottle of red mercurochrome. After kissing on the couch, we fell to the floor and managed to come several times amid the liquid that covered our skin and submerged us in an antiseptic odor. So desirable and beautiful was her body that I spent the entire night gazing at it, thanking God for that undeserved prize.

I was caressing her breasts and waist and kissing her sweet mouth when the director of the Pasteur Ward appeared with a whip in hand. That afternoon they took me to the other damned hospital and if I regret anything it was the loss of those books which had illuminated me during so many months. At the other place I ended up meeting again the Cambodian, whose hands and tongue had been cut off.

As for me, they wouldn't let me read, but I

was able to sing in the eunuch choir directed by the reverand Father Jean-Paul Bonhomme, august chaplain of that hospital where those who cannot resist the temptation of literature are sent.

The Unending Orgy of the Mannequins

THE STREETS were filled with garbage. A nauseating odor mixed with a century's aroma of urban decrepitude. On some corners the mountain of bagged detritus was six feet high. Arabs in turbans and black Nigerians secretly approached and rescued a few things from the foul confusion that reigned on the rue Faubourg du Temple. The nostalgic music of Samir escaped from a few cous-cous restaurants, bottles of Sidi-Brahim stacked beside their green doors. Late afternoon had fallen early. The December cold froze the water in the canals and the asphalt seemed covered by blocks of ice that projected a mysterious and terrifying sheen. Rheumatic old women, fat old men, and diabetics went out in quest of their baguette and a lamentation of a Celinian sadness crept down the staircases of old mansions smelling of abandoned pantries. A few neon signs began turning on and the sulfuric phosphorescent light cast itself over the asphalt and the dirty, humid, frozen walls of time.

Ben Zouzi Al Ben Azar crossed the building's

threshold and started climbing the spiral staircase that reeked with intense odor. On each landing were two numberless doors from which emanated the smell of simple, meager meals. Suddenly a blind man would come out of one of those doors accompanied by a mangy dog. Or a portly man from the Sudan would open his door, peering out with shining eyes. Or a furious woman would stick her head out to complain about the heels of the visitor's shoes. He had climbed more than ten floors before reaching the last one. Out of breath, he reached the door of #27 and knocked.

A woman dressed in a purple sweater and tight jeans answered the door and immediately opened her arms to embrace the Arab, a thin man with citrine skin, a moustache and black eyes who spoke perfect French. He rested a few minutes on the couch and then stood up and took off the Astrakhan jacket he bought at a flea market. The woman came over and let him kiss her. When night had already begun to cover the street, the woman grabbed the man's body and began kissing it as if she were devouring him. Through the half-open window most of the cold was filtered by the aquamarine light of a neon sign whose rays covered the face of the beautiful German woman. The man brought her to his body and began kissing her neck. Their bodies entwined in desperate possession and they rolled onto the floor where they quickly undressed and then took each other, pounding against the walls and messing up the cushions. A long cry, and their panting breath turned into a new silence that made way for the rumble of trucks and screeching metal doors. The radio, which had been turned on while they were making love, sounded with an announcer's voice, the smooth voice of an angel indicating where traffic was worst and what the temperature was outside. Afterward he played a song by Veronique Samson. The woman stood up to get a bottle of Cointreau, the only thing she had, and served the man a drink.

The naked woman straddled Ben Zouzi and began kissing him again. The sweat of their bodies hung in the air and the acrid odor of sex inundated the apartment until Deborah cried out again and the man gasped for air.

Someone knocked on the door. Still panting, Ben Zouzi got up and motioned for her to go into another room. His heart pounded. Deborah put on her pants and purple sweater. The man quickly dressed and then grasped his lover's hand. He took a revolver out of his jacket and pointed it at the door. They knocked again and again on the door and when it broke down there appeared two men dressed like Islamic mullahs. In an incomprehensible language they made accusations at the Arab and rushed upon him, brandishing their scimitars. Ben Zouzi didn't hesitate and shot them point blank before the fatidic blades could cut off his head. Stepping quickly over the corpses, the two fled down the steps in the blink of a eye before losing themselves in the garbage-filled streets.

Later they walked through a warehouse of dusty mannequins, a place so enormous they couldn't see where it ended. Hands, legs, feet, heads, fingers all were strewn over the floor. Torn and discarded clothing, obsolete models, high heels, wigs. Steel racks and clothing hangers. Everything covered by an intermittent neon light. A few rats hid beneath the dead mannequins. Deborah and Ben Zouzi sat and rested on a staircase. Then the man took off the woman's

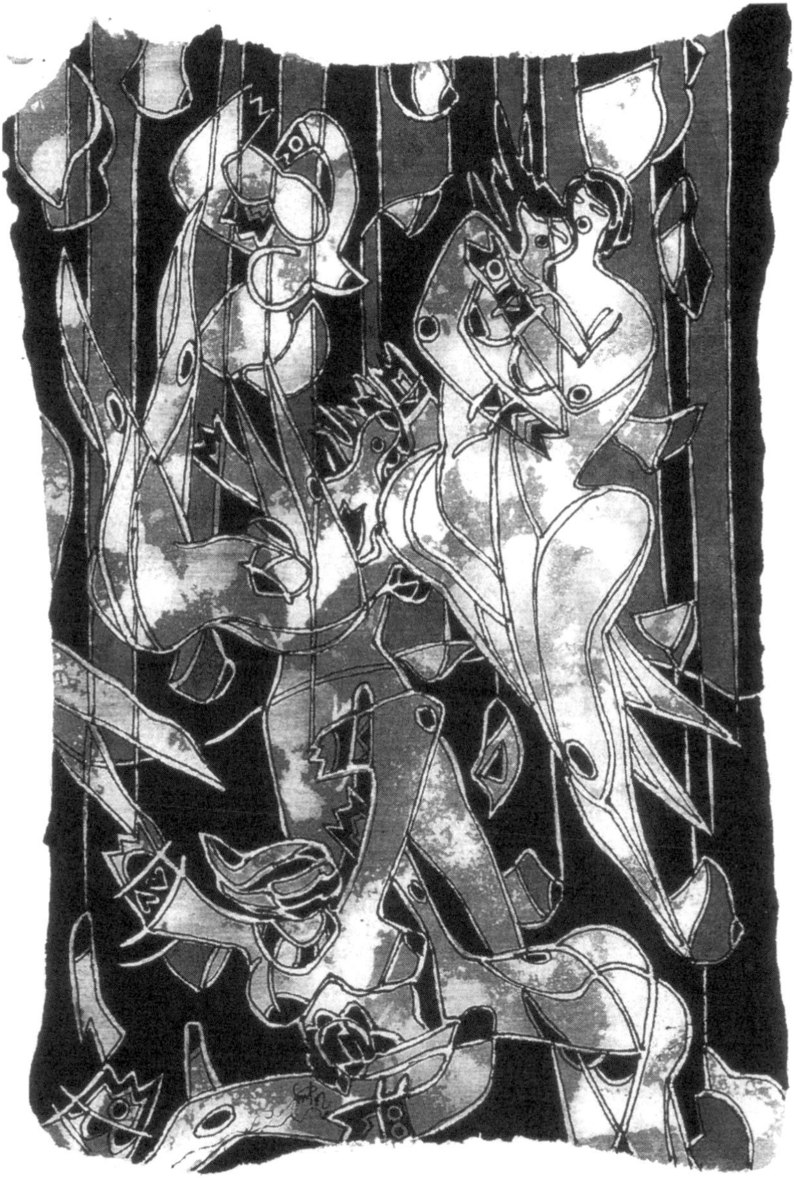

sweater and began to kiss her breasts, sucking them while she caressed his body. They rolled over the mannequins again. Naked, still sweating from their exertions, they took each other in every position, creating yet more disorder among the thousands of pallid anthropomorphic figures whose blues eyes looked on in astonishment. The lovers banged against the walls. The woman screamed and trembled, while invoking Allah the man rhythmically penetrated her. A final cry of pleasure rang throughout the entire enclosure and the eyes of the thousands of mannequins gleamed even more. The soft murmur of their hard extremities began to resound. The constant hammering of plaster increased, along with the murmur of a thousand breaths and moans. In a few moments, while the sprawling bodies of the Arab and German rested amidst them, the mannequins embraced and possessed each other with a cannibalistic fury. The succession of orgasms was unending, eternal. Nobody ever learned the final exact fate of Ben Zouzi Al Ben Azar and his luscious lover Deborah Ochs.

The First Battles of Love

AT NOON THE CAVALRY appeared and entered the campus. Whinnying on the asphalt avenue before they galloped over the paths of our dreams were spirited sorrels, ridden by brawny soldiers dressed in kepis and brandishing long sabers whose gleams bedazzled us. The city was turning gray. Large clouds from the Bogotá savanna covered the diaphanous sky caressing the students' bodies, and the rumor of catastrophe took hold of paradise. People ran to hide behind buildings or next to immense trees. Those who couldn't flee remained trapped in the buildings awaiting the soldiers, with no hope of getting out. Trembling with fear, we felt the ground shake from the galloping mounts of the barbarous Attilas of the Republic. Justice had arrived in full force to smash the windows and beat the girls screaming "Death to the president!"

Estrella ran with me alongside a soccer field. She was the most beautiful and intelligent of all the students. Long black hair shone above her flannel shirt drenched with sweat. White teeth of an Amazonian goddess gleamed in her face marked by certain proud mulatto features. Her thin delicate body, like some kind of gazelle, moved through the air, lifted by her winged tennis shoes. I had been in love with her for a long time, but had never dared talk to her. In vast sunny halls we sometimes saw each other alone and, foolish and trembling, I would gaze at her until she went out into the equatorial sun to lose herself on the avenues. Now we ran and ran, behind us other kids who vanished in the tumultuous fear. From afar we heard the first tear gas canisters and shots, so democratic that they killed without distinguishing between color or class.

It was then I realized something strange. After the crowd had dispersed we remained trapped without knowing how or why in the storeroom of the university kitchens. And even better: trembling, Estrella embraced me. The soft smell of fragrant shampoo in her hair and the lash of her beating heart completely overwhelmed me, while outside the battle had just begun. A few stones thrown from other buildings crashed through the windows, tinkling onto the mosaic floor. Later music cast itself in echoes over the stairs, agonizingly reaching us. Estrella and I lay gasping, sprawled over the sacks of rice and wheat. We had run so far that a few minutes later our hearts were bursting. Her clean torn blue jeans throbbed like her panting breath, while tears of furious joy ran down her cheeks.

I met her at a soccer game. I played defense and she played offense on the other team. Being a good athlete, she quite easily dribbled around the younger players and when she came to me I remained paralyzed, but then struggled to stop her, hoping to get even closer. There I got to know her smell and her smile, the softness of her skin and the fresh healthiness of her body. A few days later we all discovered in alarm she was married to the youngest member of the group, and they were the two happiest people on the whole campus. From that point on all the hope of those who had secretly loved her was dashed, until the day the forces of order delivered her to my arms on an afternoon that would once again turn sunny.

Estrella was the only daughter of a high-level official in the Merchant Marines, and because of his position she often had to accompany him on long missions abroad. She lived four years in Japan, three in Helsinki, one in Liverpool, six months in Gibraltar, two years in New York and one in Hamburg, where she finished high school. At eighteen she entered the Faculty of Philosophy and Letters at the university, and now, six months later, she expressed her pleasure at returning to her country from which she had been uprooted as a child.

On cold dark days she would arrive in a long woolen poncho, like those worn by peasants in the high plains; on sunny days she would wear the rustic embroidered blouses of village women who lived in distant ravines and valleys. She used to play the flute. And this was just one of her many enchantments. One festive night when we were all completely drunk, she played for us for hours unknown melodies: Japanese tunes, English folk songs, Scandinavian musical sagas and happy Mediterranean airs we all vigorously applauded.

Estrella woke from a long sleep. It was 5:30 and the slanting sun penetrated through the window that formed rectangles over the provisions dispersed throughout the warehouse. Through a megaphone we heard the calls of the army to rebel groups who were still shooting from university dormitories.

"You'll pay for the death of the horses!" they shouted from the distance. The week before several students had killed with iron rods three army horses, which were buried with full military honors in the presence of President Pombo, Cardinal Armadillo, and the Minister of Defense, General Bello Uría. The present day's incursion was done to seek revenge for the three animals. On a radio announcement coming from an unknown place, we heard that at least ten students had died during the afternoon confrontation and that the university was surrounded by army troops. President Pombo had given orders to finish off the "subversive hordes" who were putting in jeopardy "democratic institutions." Over the radio our alarmed parents requested clemency for the students caught in the army's rat trap.

Estrella and I talked for a long while, savoring the juices and canned meats we found by the thousands in that warehouse. In a corner we found two bottles of wine, no doubt left over from some cocktail party, which we drank until we got a bit drunk. The beautiful young woman seemed fascinated by the adventure and instead of being sad she arranged a bed in a corner and laying down with open arms, she recounted stories about her voyages and asked me about mine. I could only tell her about my excursions to the volcanoes and the happy nights I had spent in a mountain retreat watching it snow in the tropics. Outside the cavalry continued to pass back and forth and bullets struck against the walls. We heard explosion after explosion, mixed with voices from megaphones and military radios. Night fell and we embraced each other in the darkness. She offered her lips and hugged me, letting me drown in her scent as we slowly moved into each other.

A sudden burst of gunfire inundated the warehouse with tremendous force. There was nothing I could do. Many days later I awoke in a military hospital, turned into one monstrous wound. The only thing that lets me live is the memory of that fleeting star which night has swallowed for eternity. Her voice and her smell, her body and the certainty that at the last minute she was mine stir me on in this life full of spectators where no one is forgiven. I only lived to tell this story to those who might wish to hear it.

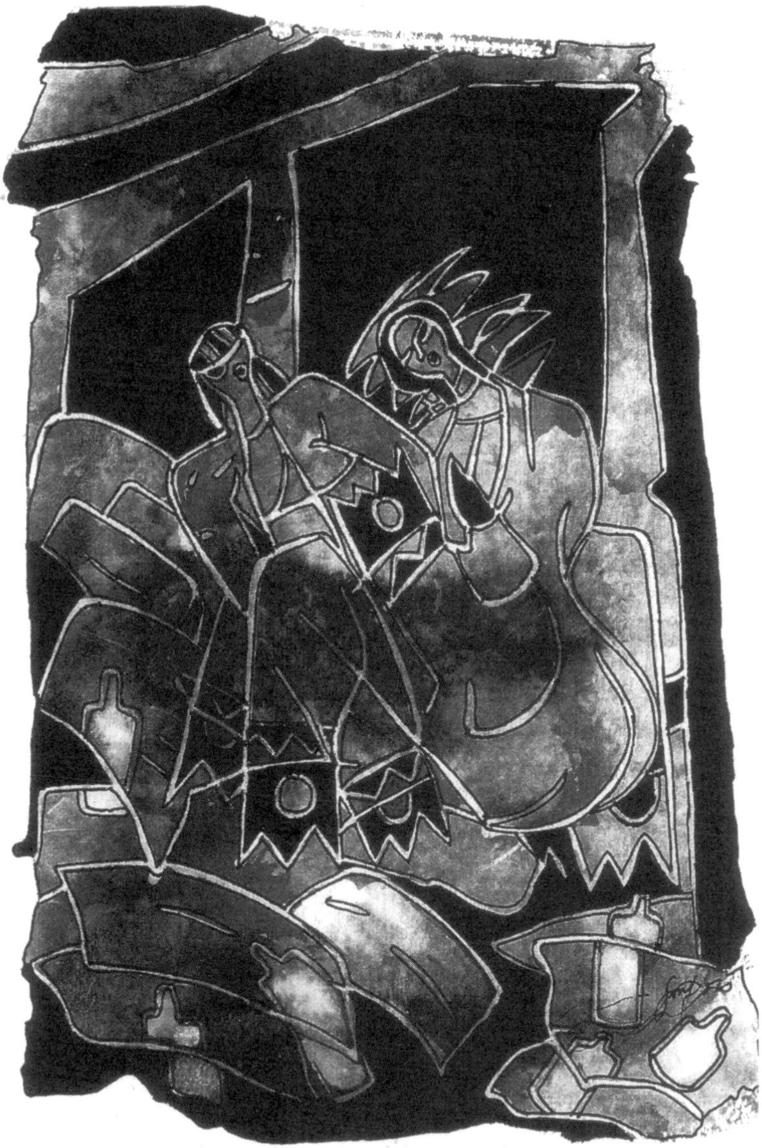

The Lady from the Depths of the Sea

A LITTLE OLD WOMAN with a canine face, slow pace, and bulging eyes descended the marble staircase of the Hotel Cimarrosa and coughed clamorously. Just before leaving her suite she'd had a run-in with one of the maids, for which her acrid mood made her look at people with infinite hate. The woman crossed the vast salon of the vintage restaurant, its walls covered with paintings of nineteenth century nobles and its floors with purple carpeting. A slight smile nevertheless appeared on her wrinkled face, over which signs of sadness and happiness, panic and felicity, had passed so many times. The old poetess, her hair all done up, headed to her table using a cane. She sat down and a new peace filled her entire body. The sun penetrated through the large windows while a violin melody wafted through the place where gathered glorious old women from the end of the century, theatre stars, poets, great and illustrious businessmen, and this or that bohemian who entertained the potentates with his eccentricities or grotesque acts.

Madame ordered a glass of absinthe. The young man, already accustomed to serving the lady the green liquid, nodded his head and returned with the cool liquor. She drank slowly, her gaze lost in the carpet, as if she were remembering her former times of glory.

Nobody there could have imagined the person possessing that diminutive body had been of one of the most desirable women of her day. Her theater, situated where the Balajo is today, near 21 rue de la Roquette, was the site of performances that would have made an inhabitant of the distant future blush.

She had founded it in the flower of her seventeenth year, when along with several beautiful friends she decided to create a spectacle that would overwhelm the good manners of her era. Dedicated to nude lesbian scenes, they managed in a few months to gather there exquisite men and unparalleled women willing to break with the rigid attitudes and constraints of their social strata.

The performance would begin in a violet penumbra, then artificial lights cast a reddish hue from behind curtains that disappeared in flashes of methylene blue. A seventeen-year-old woman dressed like a vestal virgin would appear and recite a few Saphic verses. Then she would recline upon a divan, while through other doors appeared women who surrounded the beauty and began to undress and caress her until she came in ecstasy.

The scene was fleshed out: one by one they took her in the most intimate way and in turn when the lovely thing awoke she made them die of happiness. The magic lights covered them all and then they faded away, in the end leaving just the flash of the beautiful face of the actress, the audience bursting into applause. Later in a nearby room those in attendance would join the beautiful women to drink absinthe, smoke opium and hashish, and end their evenings in long bacchanalias that no other century has yet to equal.

Madame was thinking about all this while she sipped another drink, bathed by the rays of the sun. She laughed a moment, drunkenness having already taken hold of her, and began to hum the leitmotif from that unreal spectacle. Over each of the last few days, ever since old age had taken her by surprise, she had tried to construct the past knowing that memories kill even the strongest and most powerful. In order to call death she dedicated herself to remembering, managing with her sensibility to recollect the most delicious and unforgettable sensations. Those beautiful girls who acted in the lesbian ritual at the Sapphic Theatre came to the salon and spoke with her amid the fog of decrepitude. Some of them had married shortly afterwards, having families and husbands and children, or died in debt in distant or exotic villages situated on the other side of the sea. Others were devoured early on by vice and flesh, while she remained the victim of lucidity.

Finally Madame got up and went to sunbathe at the beach. The shouts of children inundated the windy path leading to the sea. The children surrounded her and began to make her laugh. Next to the little stands selling food and drinks musicians played happy tunes. The visitors, poured into their ridiculous and puritanical bathing suits, enjoyed the afternoon. Proper ladies dressed in black conversed while their daughters in long dresses let their clothing flow in the soft caress of the sea. The reddened, almost bloody sun slowly began to proclaim its imminent departure.

The poetess, the actress, the great woman rested beside a rock and clearly felt the weight of nostalgia, the useless, desperate war old age wages with the past. Life had passed like a dream and like a dream she found herself next to the sea at the Hotel Cimarrosa, smothered with attention and luxury, without children or husband, without grandchildren, without family. Night was falling and people were leaving the beach. Madame remained there writing one last poem. Then she made a paper boat with the page she had written and threw it into the turbulent waves that began to flow back, dragging along snails, dead fish and an occasional sea star.

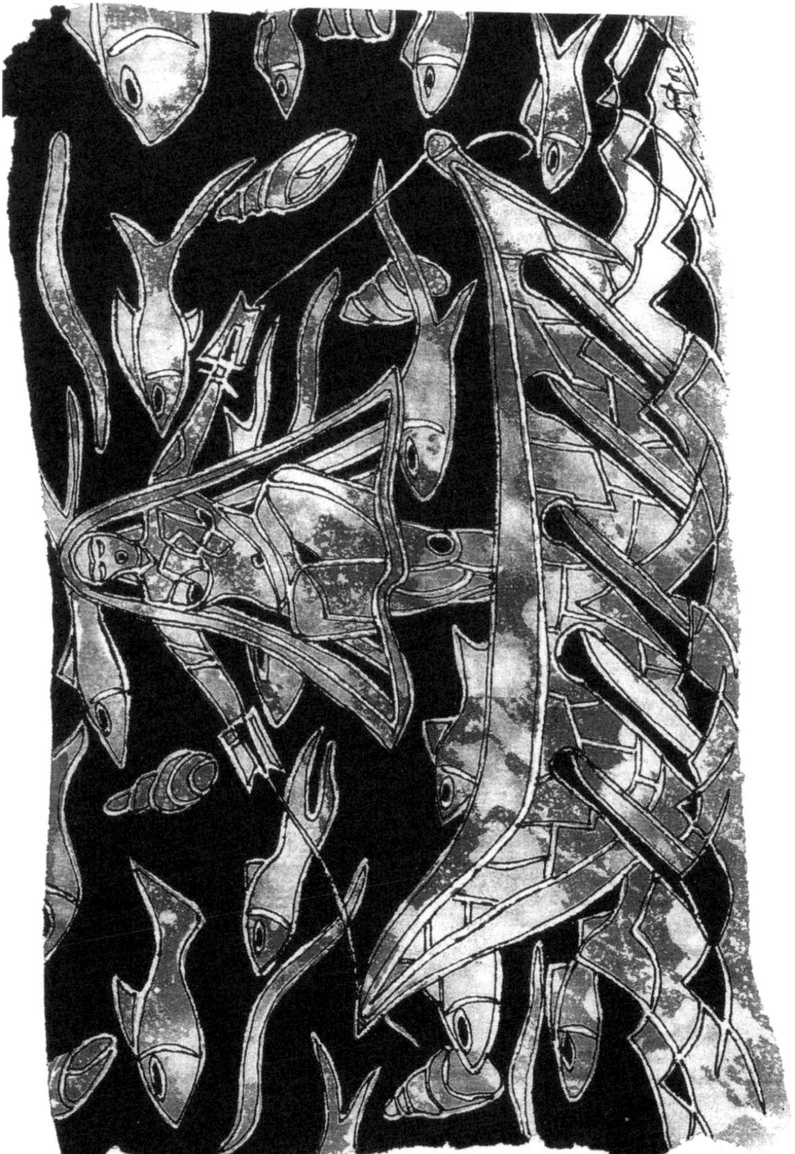

II

GARRETS AT THE END
OF THE WORLD

.

Garrets at the End of the World

THE GARRETS of marvelous cities are usually favorable territory for exercising the pleasures of the imagination. Situated on the wide corridors of sinister buildings, at the top of spiral staircases where the dying odor of time wanders, these ingenious jails stir fever and delirium. Compared to great mansions or immense apartments, the garret demands from the inhabitant a strict spatial control. And bodily contact there is easier and more exciting. A great worldwide brotherhood of garret residents exists, mostly composed of foreigners. Thus as in remote epochs the hermit lovers of hair-shirts and meditation used to hide in caverns, the modern heirs of that spiritual army choose the top-floor rooms to feed their dementia. One of these dwellers used to like to read at night Rubén Darío's poem dedicated to exalting the wolf that the saint wished to redeem by bringing into the world of men. He was a thin emaciated man with flaccid lungs and sunken cheeks. A greenish skeleton, like some kind of moribund being, he would pass the evening reciting aloud verses of the modernist poet whom he admired more than anything else in the world. His admiration for the prince of Latin American language became more intense the more he consumed immense cigarettes of hashish and loose Gitane tobacco. In the late night hours he would wander the back streets of Barcelona's Gothic quarter in search of dope dealers and procurers of vice and perversion.

One time he was walking along the city breakers and in the distant afternoon discerned a golden ship that had been refused entry to the port. A beautiful shining ship, it reflected the sun's slanting rays as its shadow spread over the Mediterranean. Sitting with a few friends on one of the rock breakers, he drank gin from a bottle and cursed the port authorities. For more than half an hour, while the sun shone ever more intensely on the hull, his obsession turned to the need of rescuing the anchored ship. Taking the last swig from the bottle, he suddenly jumped into the sea and swam a few meters against the stingy force of the water, which seemed to devour him as his friends looked on in astonishment.

But death can't snatch such beings capable of challenging the sea on the altars of image or caprice. She knows how to distinguish those who lovingly sacrifice their lives for a beautiful memory or strange adventure and thus don't really deserve the fatal blow of the Parcae, but on the contrary the scythe's indulgence and the doleful harpy's caress. This man, resident of pensions and garrets whose only capital is a black suitcase full of his book collection, has passed through the world like a phantom, from city to city, fleeing from work, from steady employment and commitment.

All we hear from him are the sporadic letters that always come from a garret different than the one to which his innumerable friends, disciples and admirers send their return letters that never reach him. Where is he now? A few people affirm they've seen him in Trieste working as a gardener for some distant relatives of Paul Morand. As proof, they offer a fabulous orchid cultivated by those old ladies that only flowers once every four years in the hothouse they adore like a sacred niche full of idols. They say he used to seclude himself there to write in the ramshackle, lugubrious warehouses of a glorious city that in its time was the crossroads of all known worlds. Other travelers have seen him while passing through Carrera, where he was working as a waiter in a hospice for Benedictine monks. The proof is a piece of marble he used to settle a debt he had with a Colombian sculptor he met in Brindisi. A geologist poet, contracted in the mercury mines of Yakutsk, said the garret hermit was seen on a whaler in the Caspian Sea in company of several Ukrainian dissidents who adopted him for a while. A few miserable beings from his country nicknamed him the "literary guest" and criticized the fact he had spent two weeks in their apartment on rue Bonaparte, in Paris, without ever picking up the check at a restaurant or bistro.

Several times he's been seen drinking coffee the entire afternoon at some dreary locale, a Trotskyite bookstore in Stockholm, where with the first paid cup he could drink refills. In Berlin they saw him working alongside Turks demolishing an old warehouse. There he fell in love with a woman who fancied Latin Americans and supported and pampered him for several weeks before he escaped to take a solitary voyage through Bulgaria and Yugoslavia. The poets from Bogotá assure he was there for a week, his eyes bulging in terror, refusing to greet his friends, and they describe the macabre rictus of his face when he watched from the hilltops the tenacious nocturnal fire at the Palace of Justice. Since then nobody has heard anymore about him and those who learned so much from his life wish for a clue to his whereabouts. His first name is Miguel and his last De Francisco, for which one can well understand his devotion to Rubén Darío's poem about the "gentle" St. Francis of Assisi. He's no more than thirty-seven, but his desire to look like the French Renaissance poet Clément Marot makes him seem a bit older. He doesn't like to drink milk and he detests oranges. He can't stand the dreary atmosphere of beach resorts and suffers from allergies to thermal baths. He thinks North American writers, including Hemingway, are stupid and abhors compromised poetry. When things were going well for him he was a regular at the restaurant Perets in Barcelona and the bar Tales in the same city, where they considered him the last, best absinthe drinker. He knows by heart entire stories and poems by the Argentine writer Jorge Luis Borges, including his poem about Chesterton's battle at Lepanto, but he gets really upset when people label him "Borgesian." He doesn't believe in revolution, or democracy, and he would love to have been a Renaissance merchant or a Portuguese traveler dedicated to doing business in the Malay Islands. Among his extravagances figures his consideration of Núñez Cabeza de Vaca the precursor of the new Latin American narrative and Spain the first country of Africa. Another of his defects is that he still likes women and hopes to convert himself into

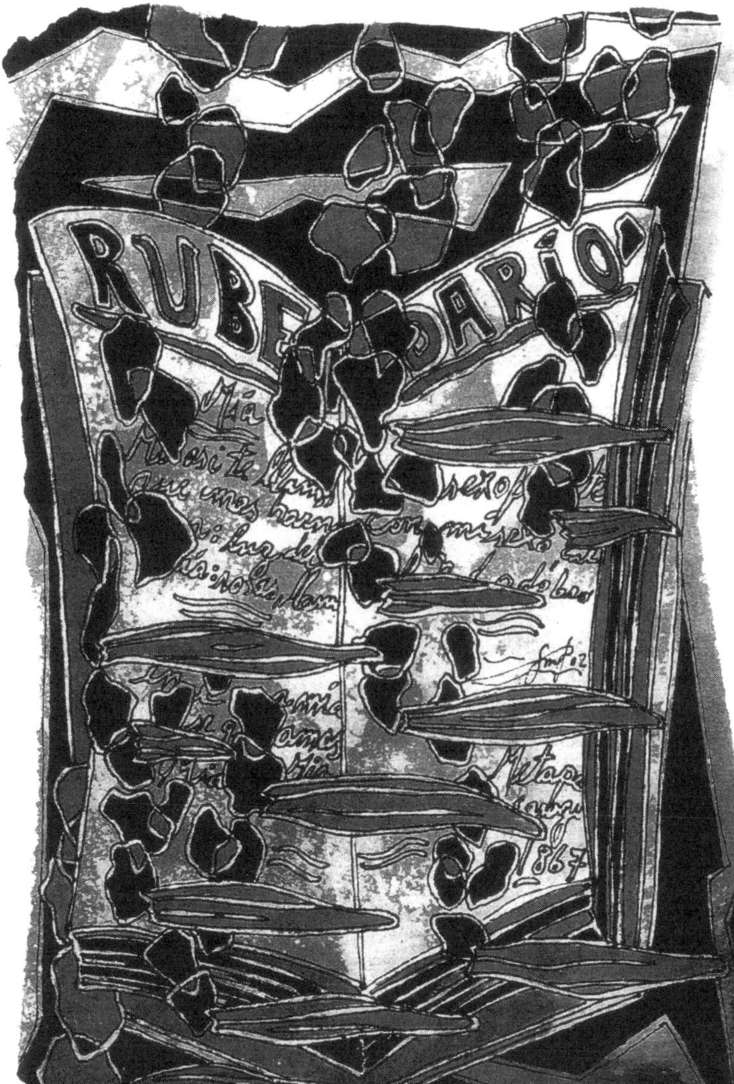
DARÍO

history's ultimate heterosexual. He doesn't wear blue jeans or leather jackets; he prefers pants of woven fabric, blue shirts, black shoes and purple socks. As a child he dreamt of being a high prelate in the Catholic Church and for a while contemplated becoming the first Latin American pope. He drinks Coca-Cola and his favorite women are Lauren Bacall and Mia Farrow. He hates Woody Allen and Julio Iglesias. He's never voted in his life nor does he ever consider doing so. He likes rock and Chopin, Rubens and Paul Klee, Senegalese music and spaghetti. He once talked to Julio Cortázar. He considers Cioran a philosopher for withered old men and has never read a book of sociology. Some people think he died in a car accident, others suppose he entered an orthodox monastery in Greece, although I'm inclined to believe he's a collective invention of the garret dwellers. From having imagined him so much, they've ended up converting themselves into his replica, wandering through the world attempting to create him and so give solace to readers, skeptics and pot smokers.

Between Snow and the Tomb

MY BEST FRIENDS from youth became in time a high-ranking military officer, a Benedictine monk, and a mad poet. Since that time each one seems to have lived out the ultimate destiny of his days. The soldier was once a strong, authoritarian young man full of prowess who enjoyed forcing the weakest to put on the most lamentable spectacles. One time lashing a whip he made a wimpy little lad carry a cross of rough-hewn timbers made from the lumber of a recently felled tree. A fancier of fencing and the pentathlon, this future army gorilla knew well that despite his taste for literature, his final destiny would be the barracks or perhaps the presidency, obtained by the force of bullets and blood.

As for the second, everything seemed to indicate his fate would be the cassock of some exquisite order whose tradition has been vigorously established throughout the centuries. But he was nothing like the swordsman: pallid, middling in height, myopic and a little effeminate, this friend, a desperate reader of

German, Greek and Russian classics who plunged into studies of philosophy and psychology, chose the cassock to flee from terrestrial sin. He couldn't stand that despite being made of angelic matter, desire dragged him into obscure allies where he devoted himself to what he once censured as abject and degrading. Only true sanctity could save him from such despised dissolution, from that perdition which leads common men toward a living death. Perhaps he was wrong and his perdition in the solitude of the monastery, far from indecent luxury, was a most clear metaphor of human usury. Possessed by imaginary dreams called forth by satanic shadows, my friend will suffer in life like no one else and end thus his brief sojourn through the world of earthly beings.

The third has traced with his maddened gaze the fleeting destiny of a shooting star. Hedonist, eccentric, exhibitionist, this specimen of poetry gave loose rein to attaining his dearest illusion: realizing all his desires. With regard to literature, no doubt he was the best read of the three, not so much because his culture and erudition equaled the future Benedictine's, but because of the manner in which he gave himself over to creation. From the time he was an adolescent, really just a child, he wrote almost daily letters, articles and long poems in every manner and style and read books at random ranging from Bossuet's sermons to Apollinaire's *Les Onze Mils Verges*, from *The Imitation of Christ* by Thomas à Kempis to *Tropic of Cancer* by the ineffable Henry Miller. Those who knew him had no doubt he would become someone great, but his hellish city, the fact of being such a contrarian and having sunk to the very bottom without finding a grip, love or credo, led him irremediably toward the prideful reign of madness. The last time I saw him he was passing down Central Avenue walking an incredibly beautiful Dalmatian, not stopping to acknowledge those who looked at him with smiles or hate. Thus every late afternoon he went out from the mansion he had inherited from his parents, where he lived amidst luxury, to wander through public places dressed like a nineteenth-century dandy, sometimes half-nude, other times in sandals and a tunic, cursing the massive sacred structures and the buildings of progress. He lies now, they say, in a ward at the Santa Clara insane asylum, on the banks of a raging tropical river in his hot and idolatrous city.

The four of us would sometimes go to the edge of death. My friend the future army gorilla, after having just turned sixteen, once talked us into climbing the peaks of the mountain range near the snowy slopes of the volcano of Girardot. A few nights earlier, after drinking aguardiente and smoking marihuana and listening to a guitar recital by one of his father's friends, he told us that literature, the reason for our friendly meetings, had to be taken into the terrain of adventure. We had to demonstrate our valor by climbing snowy mountains and hiking through arid deserts for a few days so we might exorcise the ardent heat of our valley city.

At first there was a certain censuring of the project on the part of the future monk, whose name was Carlos Durandarte. He implied it was a vainglorious proposal, but in the end the vote was a landslide in favor of the adventure. Everything was all prepared when another friend who had been gone, Francisco Noreña, returned from Boston. At an early age he already had the profile of a future politician, no doubt a

74

senator or at least a cabinet minister, due to his intelligence, his astonishing oratorical capability and his poetic skill. Francisco went with us that morning to the heights of the most feared volcano of the time.

Michel the soldier, Carlos Durandarte the monk, Rodrigo Adonaís the poet, Francisco the politician, and I reached the edge of the icy desert around four in the afternoon. There sat an abandoned mansion that in other times was a storehouse for potatoes and a rest stop for dangerous muleteers. At the time of our adventure it was already quite in ruins, but it had a roof, garrets and rooms visited from to time by certain birds from the land of perpetual snows. Up to that point everything had gone well. The trip had been hard, but enjoyable; we walked through beautiful prairies full of pure-bred bulls; we hiked around the edge of thermal lakes that reflected the lost gray clouds, we collected highland plants, some of which had flowers like the edelweiss of the Romantics, and we talked about literature, religion, politics, love and war on the edge of precipices overlooking roaring waterfalls. Never in our lives would we five forget that day, when in our youth and joy we were closer to happiness and glory than we had ever been.

As the afternoon passed, the temperature fell unmercifully and shortly afterward we were all, except for Michel, nearly moribund, freezing, unable to speak and hoping to die. I only remember the penumbra of the night, illuminated by the moonlight cast over the immense snowy mountains. The future monk managed to get up and vomit from the loft, while the poet and politician tried to warm each other with their bodies inside a torn sleeping bag. As for me, there was a moment when my temples pounded as if they would burst, while in that delirium I heard the future captain's imprecations against our weakness: "Don't die, you assholes!" he shouted loudly, trying to hide the fact he too had already become victim to the cold.

At dawn we were rescued by a military jeep that happened to pass by. We were all alive, except for Francisco Noreña. Now, over the distance of time, each of us will remember him and others far away. Each of us will carry his own fateful destiny, but in that fearful moment, when the dead come back from the netherworld to greet us, we won't be able to forget how we are joined forever in that zone which crackles between fiction and life or madness and dreams.

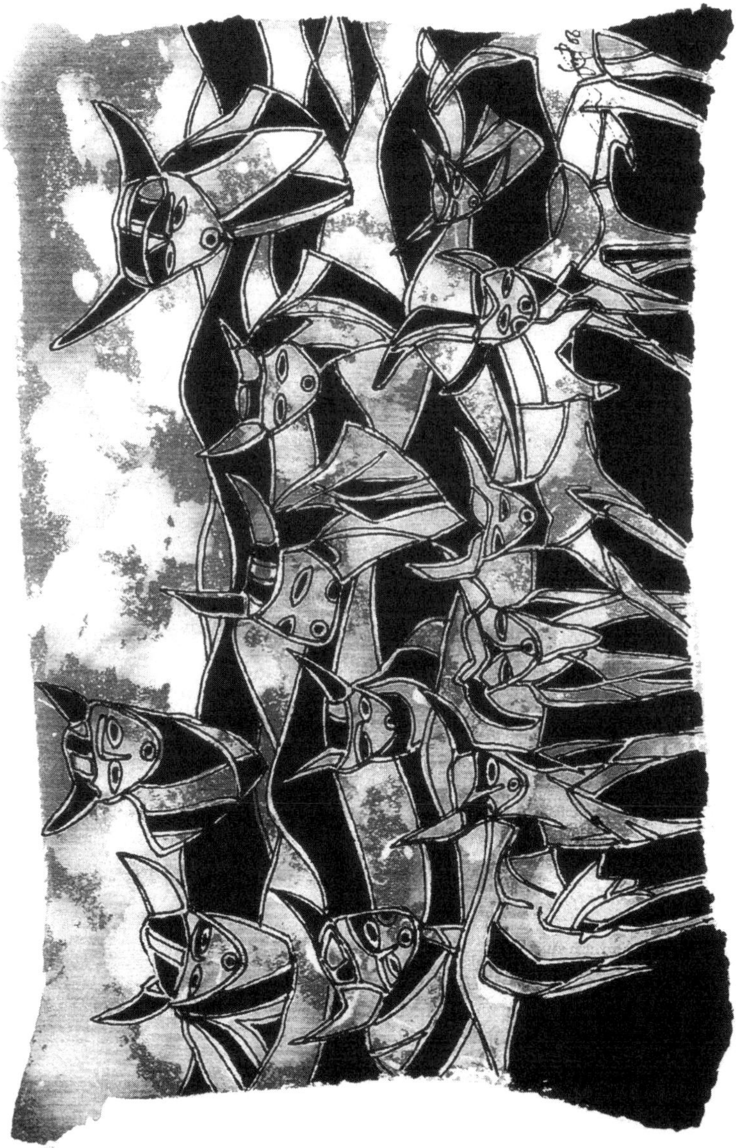

Frankenstein, the Arabs and Us

A GROUP OF YOUNG people was peacefully walking down the rue Saint-André-des-Arts when an Arab approached pretending to be a police officer and asked the South Americans for some identification. One of them who had recently run into trouble with the authorities due to false accusations of drug trafficking immediately insulted the Moroccan, whom he pushed after seeing they were dealing with an impostor. He found it despicable that an Arab would try to feign the racist tactics of the French police. At first it didn't seem like anything much, but the supposed cop slapped Oscar in the face, and the latter was about to respond when a Gallic patrol car appeared on the rue Saint Jacques. Knowing they would all end up on the losing side if they were detained, they pretended to converse amicably while the sleepwalking authorities passed by. When the patrol car disappeared toward Chatelet, they tangled in a fist fight soon joined by other North Africans.

    I was carrying in my hands the two volumes

of Mary Wollstonecraft Shelley's correspondence, which I had just bought in a used bookstore for a laughable price. At one point in the scuffle one of the books fell to the ground and the Arab picked it up to hit Diego Cruz in the face. A little thread of blood came from the nose of my friend, who leaned against an old wooden portal. He never imagined the letters of the author of *Frankenstein* would be destined to be used as a weapon by a man of the desert.

That night we were all quite drunk. The scenes of confrontation between the Arabs and the South Americans seemed like they were lifted from some clever film. The streets reflected filaments of orange, violet, blue and red lights spreading like hyena shrieks over the street. The nocturnal fog descended from the gray mass of the sky and attached itself to the windows of old mansions, while a hot and dirty vapor emerged through the cracks of the doors. From the depths of the catacombs, converted into bars that played exotic melodies, came an indefinable, indifferent music dominated by the repeating beat of the bass and percussion. A few Greek establishments squeezed between the walls still served the disconcerted nocturnal lovers or solitary people who went out in search of someone and waited next to the Nervalian lamp posts that had survived the catastrophe of progress. The combatants' shadows moved in slow motion under the influence of a bottle of Jack Daniels. In the midst of the delirium of blows we all seemed projected onto a bottomless screen, as cold and obscure as reality.

That afternoon we South Americans had met in an alley that came out onto the banks of the Seine. A few of us had just seen a Humphrey Bogart movie,

"The Big Sleep," and others a film about the Expressionist painter Edvard Munch. A bottle emerged from the pocket of a languid-faced poet who looked like Clément Marot, and passed from hand to hand in some kind of ritualistic dance. The river scintillated in a long and sinuous reflection of light and the monuments looked like cardboard silhouettes cast upon a deep blue background. The boats of eccentric Englishmen and Danes rocked and beat against the river's containment walls. In a few of these capricious dwellings certain lovers made love in darkened rooms, by candlelight, above the murmur of the sleeping waters. The poet began to create poems and speak unconnected words and the group of South Americans began to improvise long Modernist litanies in a delicious competition of language that seemed to go on forever. The poet took from his jacket a femur and lifting it to the heavens continued creating poems that praised the spires of Gothic churches or the uselessness of the Tour Saint-Jacques. The femur's shadow spread over the waters and with absolute impunity we all understood that this marvelous city belonged more to us than to its historical owners.

Later we continued on our way down the quay, swigging new gulps from the enormous bottle. We came to a bridge lit by street lamps and sang a few songs to withstand the wintry cold. There was a fascinating moment before that river of suicides, filled with mournful stories about bedraggled people whose livid faces slowly sink into the waters while they look into the infinity of fiction. That river which has been witness to the centuries. To merchants from afar anchored there selling casks swollen with wine. To wandering artists, jesters and harlequins, clowns and comedians in make-up telling stories. To fugitives condemned to death. To leprous beggars and syphilitics who displayed their ulcers amid a lamentation of luxurious weeping.

The poet climbed out onto a ledge on the bridge and began to balance over the abyss. A tense air surrounded the rest of the South Americans, who wrapped up in their old coats of pallid sheepskin or jackets of soft leather began scolding the drunken poet. Then he moved to the aileron, where the waters fell to the river fifty feet below. He sat down there and tapped his feet to the tune of a lullaby. Oscar, a taciturn youth (who would later get beat up by the Arab) did the same and sat down next to the poet. They spoke about the weather, chance, absurd decisions, death, and then they started playing a game of a tug-of-war that drove us all crazy. The first to be thrown off would force the other to accompany him.

Under the liquor's influence, I decided to melt into the river night, to be another strangled being whose marble face would smile through the centuries. I had never seen death so close up and possible, converted into a game between two drunken youths. Oscar agreed to play and we heard a sound behind us. "Get off there, get off there!" shouted someone once and then again, and with a deliberate voice imploring us to be careful came a beautiful girl with long black tresses who tussled our hair and offered us cigarettes. All that was missing was a soulful sound for one of them to initiate the macabre dance of death. I saw the voluminous waters and held the tomes of Mary Wollstonecraft's correspondence tightly to my chest, as if they were a life preserver for a jump into the void of nothingness.

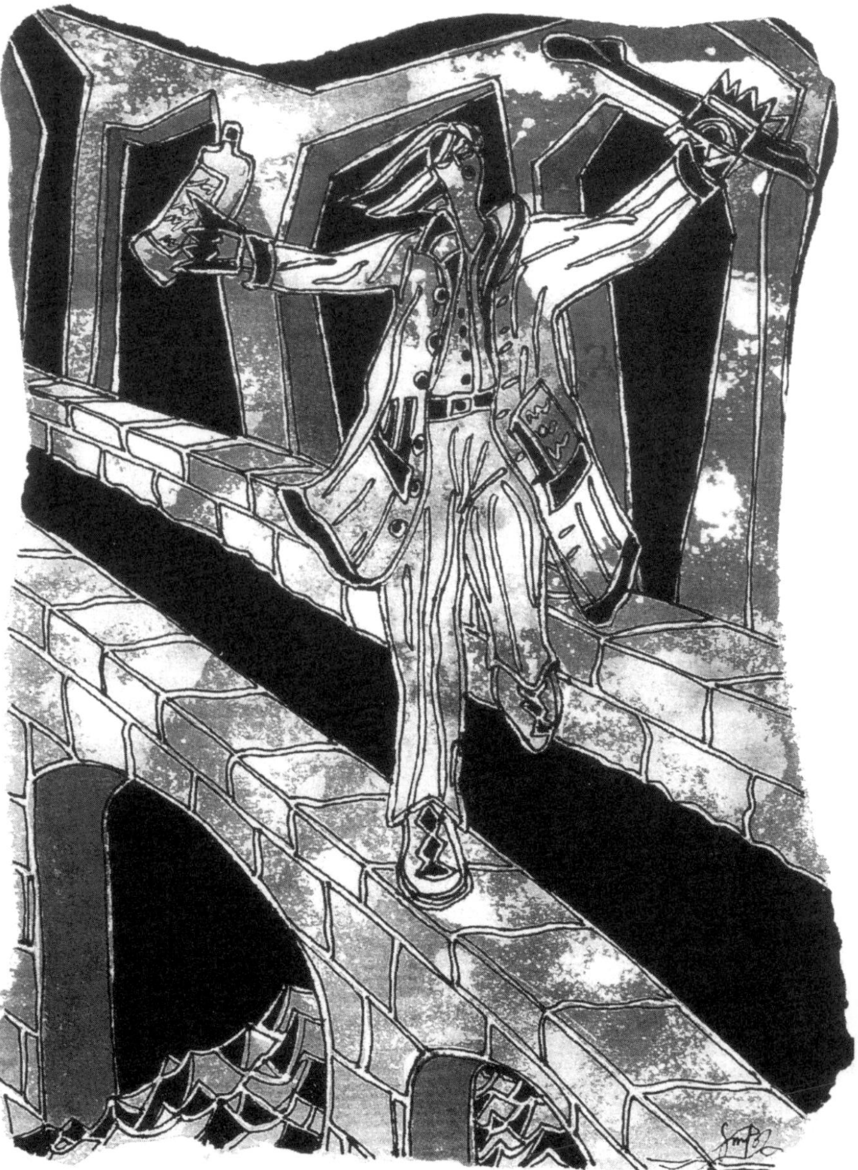

Soon it was all over. There wasn't sufficient motive to put an end to time. Perhaps there lacked a golden boat anchored far from the wharves that would make one throw himself onto the rocks of forgetfulness and challenge the salty undertow of the Atlantic.

We paused briefly in the middle of the street. We lifted the wounded youth. We ran a few meters. Then from out of the darkness other Arabs began to emerge, with their dull citrine skin, their thick accents, their little moustaches beneath broad noses. In the distance shone the blade of a scimitar. Without much consternation and in a silent complicity, almost as if of common accord, they began beating us up. A few of us writhed upon the ground, others were thrown through windows, three of them kicked me against a stinking wall, and then another took his revenge out on me. We awoke when the poet, who had hidden the femur in his jacket pocket, came back to us lamenting our bad luck and begging forgiveness, for his running away was justified, according to him, by his dedication to poetry.

We lay strewn about the alley like marionettes. The street began to empty. Somebody on the other side of the night turned off the camera projecting the scene. With their bloody noses the South Americans lost themselves among the streets and their memories continued wandering down the avenues of the world, holding onto the hand of Frankenstein and Mary Wollstonecraft Shelley.

Last Jazz in San Francisco

BLACKS, HISPANICS, whites, drug addicts, dope dealers, beggars all composed the atmosphere of Leavenworth Street, which emerged onto Market, an area filled with cheap hotels and boarding houses, Chinese and Italian restaurants and hamburger stands where you could eat for pennies. Not far off were better neighborhoods facing the bay or the classic downtown full of streetcars and modern office buildings.

The Bostonian Phil Glendenen lived there. Not in Sausalito or Berkeley, but in a run-down hotel on Market Street for which he paid a paltry rent. He was thirty-eight, but seemed much older. The man had been one of San Francisco's most furious hippies and he would take you smiling to places where Janis Joplin got tattooed or some rock star overdosed. Bald, gray-eyed, somewhat robust, he always wore tennis shoes and a black trench coat to protect himself from the fierce winds that blew down the streets and penetrated right to your bones.

For some time he had been writing a novel. In

his room next to a portable typewriter were plastic crates that contained the endless versions of his work. Like thousands of North American writers, even more solitary and forgotten than the Latin Americans, he wrote with a certain faith in art, but without any hope of convincing an editor and much less of obtaining the success of Norman Mailer or Gore Vidal. His work discussed the wanderers of the United States, those sad old hippies who had seen their illusions fail when it was already impossible to go back and remake their life. The characters were intelligent beings, too lucid perhaps, characterized by the inability to adapt themselves to the world of their time and who sooner or later ended up living in the dirty old hotels of madmen, where they chewed without bitterness on the failure of their lives. Glendenen belonged to that race of marginalized philosophers: he didn't know how to drive, he had been divorced several years earlier and still received from his ex-wife a Christmas gift wrapped in delicate pink ribbons. He didn't have any children, never ever wore a tie, was horrible at business and only knew how to smoke hashish, read, and write ongoing chapters that would end up in their plastic crates.

I began to appreciate him one day when he brought me a bag of peanuts, a hardboiled egg and an orange at the office where we worked. He had heard the rumor I hadn't been paid and was penniless. That afternoon we walked down Market Street completely high. In that office we all lived stoned on something and when the boss turned his back or took off for a while, the employees hid behind the walls of forms and statistics in order to inhale the smoke which helped them withstand another hour of their lives. In such a state we went over U.S. Census Bureau forms or spoke on the phone with those people who hadn't filled in the blanks correctly with the necessary data.

I commented to Glendenen that it had been an infernal afternoon. Around three o'clock instead of Ludwig Svoboda, a resident of Franklin Street, a strange apparatus had answered me that spoke for him in a terrifying metallic, distressed voice, like some kind of extraterrestrial being. It slowly responded to the questions I asked, leaving behind a rusty trace and between its phrases sounded the sharp flash of an obturator, the anguishing screech of a machine. I turned pale and my colleague at the desk in front of mine, Marin Bai, a thirty-five-year-old woman who dressed like Buffalo Bill and caressed me beneath the table, had to offer me a cup of coffee to calm me down.

On the phone was an old woman who instead of responding to my questions (How many people live in your house? What is your monthly income? Sex? Race? etc.) decided to recount to me how in her youth she had slept with General McArthur on some Asian island, shortly before he married his famous spouse. "He was a real man, you know." she said, "After forty years I still can't forget him...We lay down by a palm tree and did it nine times in a row. He used military condoms and his kisses burned more than the Polynesian sun..." She went on for more than half an hour and I couldn't get rid of her.

Glendenen laughed on the wet street, while in the distance the moon rose over San Francisco Bay. Stoned blacks, transvestites, Latinos, white junkies came and went from the hamburger stands and lost themselves in the allies. In a few enormous tubes in a plaza slept the exhausted beggars who drank rubbing

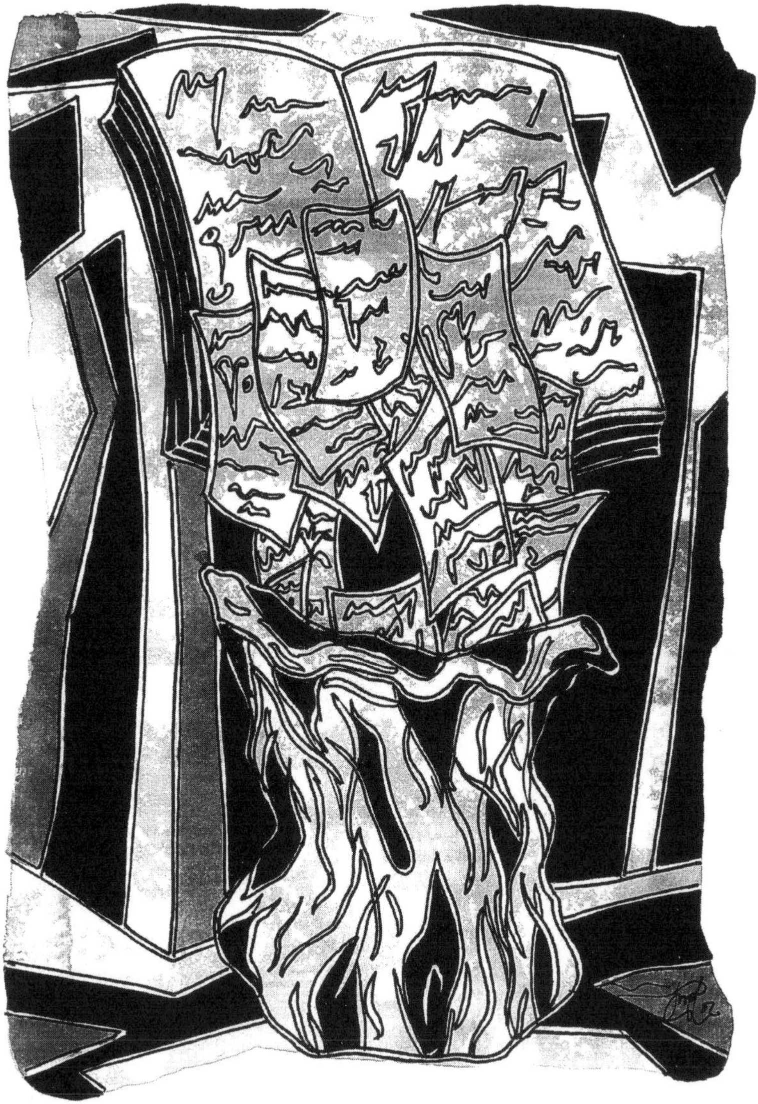

alcohol or wine and smoked cigarette butts. From a few dance clubs came the music of Ocean Express and from others the strident sounds of The Dead Kennedies or Sigmund Freud or Charanga Flórez and next to some steps came the voice of a beautiful, slender, slight half-naked Chinese woman offering her services for a few dollars. The pointed tower downtown illuminated the gray sky with an intermittent phosphorescent light. Patrol cars quickly passed by and we headed toward Mission Street. The novelist gently rolled another joint and inhaled it with an extraterrestrial pleasure. He laughed when I said "well" because according to him I was saying "whale."

"Moby Dick, Moby Dick!" he said to me, pointing with his finger out to sea. Then he burst into laughter without realizing he was one of his own characters, without understanding he wasn't a real person but a fiction in the middle of the mysterious city streets. One day he disappeared as if by magic and nobody ever heard any more of him. Phil Glendenen exists, no doubt, but it's difficult to know if his own novel devoured him, as frequently happens to writers, or if his life was saved by the God of fiction, whose labor is as fictitious as life itself or mournful as a sad jazz tune.

Chronicle of Guatemala

IT TOOK A LONG TIME for the bus to reach the outskirts of Guatemala City before taking the road to Antigua, the legendary ancient capital of the Mayan lands. The suburban streets were patrolled by police dressed in blue who looked like they were waiting for some terrorist act or pursuing some clandestine group, or were simply imposing an ominous presence in neighborhoods susceptible to uprisings. Through the bus windows caked with dirt could be seen cliffs and dusty streets leading to old run-down adobe houses, their windows and doors painted blue. There was a delay, too, from the quarrelling bus drivers who fought among themselves for the potential passengers. Their driver struggled a few blocks with another bus, passing it and then quickly managing to avoid the collision his colleague tried to force. But at one furious moment the other driver came up with a steel bar and began beating the bumper. Finally some people held back the exasperated guy and asked him to calm down, and then the bus began again slowly crawling into traffic, taking the highway to Antigua which they reached an hour later.

It was cold and everything was covered by clouds. The large stone houses truly seemed survivors of the centuries. Moss grew next to the portals and in the esplanade near the artisans market it was apparent how Antigua wasn't a city, some contemptible village, but a place charged with centenary forces, the living ruins of a secret empire. He had never felt anything like it. To walk down the cobblestone streets, to sit at a food stand and have a Coke, to cross through a little park, to buy postcards and change dollars in a bank that had once been an old mansion, he couldn't avoid feeling he was in a mossy classical terrain. Death hovered everywhere. In the market, where everyone looked unhappy from the lack of customers, the vendors said business was no longer any good, just a few Europeans and "invisible" gringos—invisible because they neither understood nor were affected by what went on here—dropping by the market from time to time to buy leather products or exotic colorful embroidered shirts, fleeing from the unemployed guides who like Calcutta beggars pursued them for a few coins. The distant mountains appeared through a strange bluish green pigment, brushed there by a magician upon a limitless cloudy, cold horizon pressed down by the rough gray air. Antigua carried its name like a curse and out of this murky atmosphere he returned hours later in the same broken down bus he had come on.

After he ate until almost bursting, he took a walk around the immense central plaza of Guatemala City, adorned by the Presidential Palace and the Cathedral, in front of which they sold delicious steaming tamales. Later he went to a concert by Flash Back and Terracotta performed that night at the Palace of Fine Arts. He had an appointment there with the envoy of a revolutionary organization from the mountains of Quiché to whom he was to hand over three thousand dollars. A long line entered the theatre, passing through a gloomy, dusty lobby leading to the immense theatre of wooden seats and dizzying walls that looked as if nobody had thought of repainting them in the last thirty years. He looked at the young people, at the nice little children of Guatemala City eating hamburgers before the show began. Standing out among them all were the boys who hugged their blond peasant girlfriends that swarm like queens in a city of Indians. With an air of self-importance, dressed in American-style clothing, but of bad taste, the blond girls were gazed upon by the entire audience as if they were mythic sirens who had fallen into the cheap seats. Because he was to speak to no one, he had time to look around and began feeling disgusted by the terrible atmosphere. He had been told that at the end of the show a man in a brown leather jacket, red neckerchief, and a gold ring with a ruby would come up beside him.

The show was worthy of a Dracula film. The rock bands jumped around in front of some badly drawn phosphorescent cardboard mushrooms. When they finished their last song the lights came up and butterflies fell from the ceiling onto the horrendous stage. Then the teen idol Leonel Flores came out and introduced a Californian flutist wearing an extravagantly flowered shirt.

After the show he slowly headed toward the exit. At first he didn't see anyone but the mass of the audience, silently moving off in the crepuscular twilight of Sixth Avenue. A few minutes passed and he

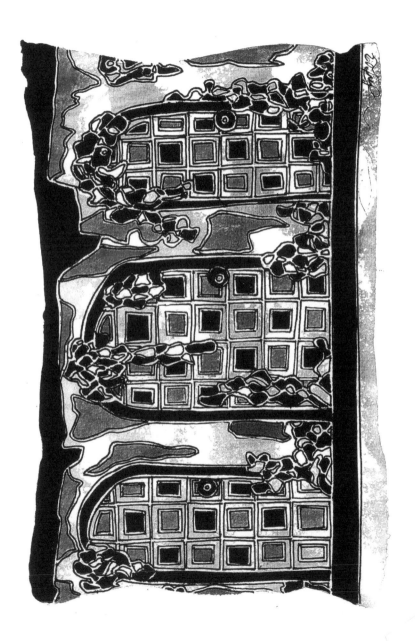

still hadn't made contact with the person to whom he was supposed to give the money. A few band members stood outside talking loudly. Then he saw his contact walking toward him on the sidewalk in front of the theatre. He suddenly saw, too, a motorcycle come around the corner with someone firing a machine gun at the man, who immediately fell to the ground. A burst of blood exploded over the street. The moribund, sanguine, violet afternoon fell over the city, while livid and trembling he moved away from the scene of the crime, fading into the somber crowd of terrorized onlookers.

Dialogue with Vultures

A FEW VULTURES fly over the river of black lava that flows down the mountain like demonic vomit. They slowly descend and come to rest upon lunar rocks and with their inquisitorial beaks cautiously observe my movements. Shortly after getting out of the taxi I understand these strange animals to be the most advantaged, the most gainful in this mournful and allegorical epoch. Old vehicles pass on the highway raising a punctual, poisonous dust that settles over the human remains recently devoured by black birds. The man leads me over the rocks toward the hollows most populated by the skulls and rib cages of civilians and soldiers.

Above us I see the long black river of volcanic lava, and a Luciferian feeling stirs me to poke beneath the brambles and thickets and prod even further among rusty belt buckles and pelvic bones covered by cobwebs. The photographer kicks a skull with the point of his shoe and places it among the others to get a good picture, while I stop to observe the bones of so many people. Among the remains are bones of dogs and skeletons of children. The smell of death floats in the wind. Ten meters away men with lost, ghost-like gazes unload refuse from a truck and observe us with curiosity, as if we were another even more rapacious kind of vulture.

The afternoon lingers in a leaden stupor and a silvery air spreads over the sterile landscape of the Killing Fields. Leaping over the stones spewed many decades ago by a nearby volcano, I destroy the extensive cobwebs and continue watching the spectacle. At times I'm struck by the temptation to clutch one of the skulls and ask the photographer to take a portrait of me with this terrible black profundity in my hand, but then I think how obscene that would be. I establish a dialogue with the furtive gazes of the vultures, while the Basque photographer continues arranging the skeletons and the taxi driver talks to me about death. He lives a few kilometers away and makes his living taking Western scavengers to see and enjoy the Killing Fields.

At times I feel like many eyes are watching me, and I discern their brilliance coming from beneath the rocks and in the air, for they fly languidly, expectantly. A thousand eyes in the skies looking at me without hate, without smiles, only looking. I feel like I've been placed in a black hollow, in one of those centers where the mass, the volume of truth is even more present than in the streets. I, too, am a piece of death. I've come here to provoke death. So it will speak to me. So it will quit me of my fear.

A plane flies through the cloudless blue sky and several vehicles, full of living men who seem as if they were already dead, pass down the highway. The taxi driver speeds up and talks to me about the towns and markets we pass through.

I feel like I'm inside an illuminated steel tube and I hear explosions in the air, invisible blasts of wind, the violent sucking of a gigantic and lascivious mouth. As we approach the City of Death that concussion of wind sways us even more, crowding out the silence. We reach the hotel on the Boulevard of Heroes and the taxi finds a place in front of the door. I walk across the carpet, ask for my key and then head to the restaurant.

An American journalist, skinny, spare, dressed casually, crosses the room with a bottle of whiskey in his hand, his lips dried and chapped. Another reporter struts about in his clogs, jeans, t-shirt and bullet-proof vest. Off to the side an obsessed and obese newsman wears a shirt an American is selling that says, "Don't shoot. I'm a journalist."

I feel like puking on the luxurious platter they serve me and the white wine tastes like a lichen extract. The sepulchral music echoing around a few businessmen stuns me. Gigantic gringo marines approach the bar and outside a man butts his heads against the wall. He looks like the soldier with a scar along one side of his face who gave me my safe conduct pass so I could freely move throughout this city of fateful ambushes. With that piece of paper I've gone through markets and alleys of lost neighborhoods and seen the faces of women crying before the tomb of an assassinated archbishop, I've seen the fear in the gaze of those who leave letters at the post office or the fear of people on the street when huge trucks filled with soldiers rumble by, their smiles menacing anyone who dares look them in the eyes.

As the days pass I begin to feel a tickling in my armpits and return to the bottle like a shipwrecked sailor does to a lifejacket. The fear of dying struck by a stray bullet or in the middle of a skirmish provoked by the army on a street corner while I drink a cup of coffee or buy a newspaper keeps me from sleeping, disturbs my mind at the moment I begin to write the articles I must send by cables and mysterious airwaves to the other side of the world, to the City of Peace. As soon as I write a few lines a bitter taste lodges in my throat that prevents me from going on. From the other side of the telex a desperate voice asks me for macabre, bloody news. But I only manage to see the scarred face of the major with a revolver in his hand holding out to me the long safe conduct pass, some lost hippies, a few hostages, the highway and a certain nostalgia for an innocent world. I enter the bar with the Basque photographer and get drunk while rock music plays, forgetting that I am an abundantly wise vulture. As the liquor induces its effects, the light becomes more tenuous and only a red haze is cast over the walls. A dance of devils surges from the depths of the stage. The waiters smile and excuse themselves, coming and going amid the clamor. In a flash the red light changes to neon and at the tables I see only vultures, buzzards who drink from the cups of the clients. On stage, instead of a band playing pop music there are birds as big as human beings, with large beaks and dark eyes whose brilliance reflects off the bottles. Their grotesque dance leaves behind a wake of feathers.

I flee toward the carpeted vestibules of the luxurious hotel and I see only uniformed vultures who help put baggage in the elevators and enormous vultures tipping a few female birds that cackle in the lobby, singing along to the solemn nocturnal melodies. I ask for the key to my room and I go up agitated, trying to fend off the images assaulting me.

A slight earthquake shakes the corridors of the sixth floor. Several shots ring from outside, far away, and murmurs from a room fly through the clean passages where a few plastic plants wither as I walk by. I search for the keys to my room and try to open it after a long interval that clumsy shaking hands make more difficult. At last I manage to open the door and enter. I take a breath and as I head with closed eyes toward the comfortable recess I need not open them to understand someone is watching me. Opening my eyelids I see an enormous nest with three chicks being fed by a vulture just my size. I raise my hands and scream and fall silent to discover my wings of black plumage flapping, casting new shadows upon the walls, my screams coming not from my mouth but from a rapacious, malodorous beak. In silence I fling myself down in the nest and there I sleep with no other hope but death.

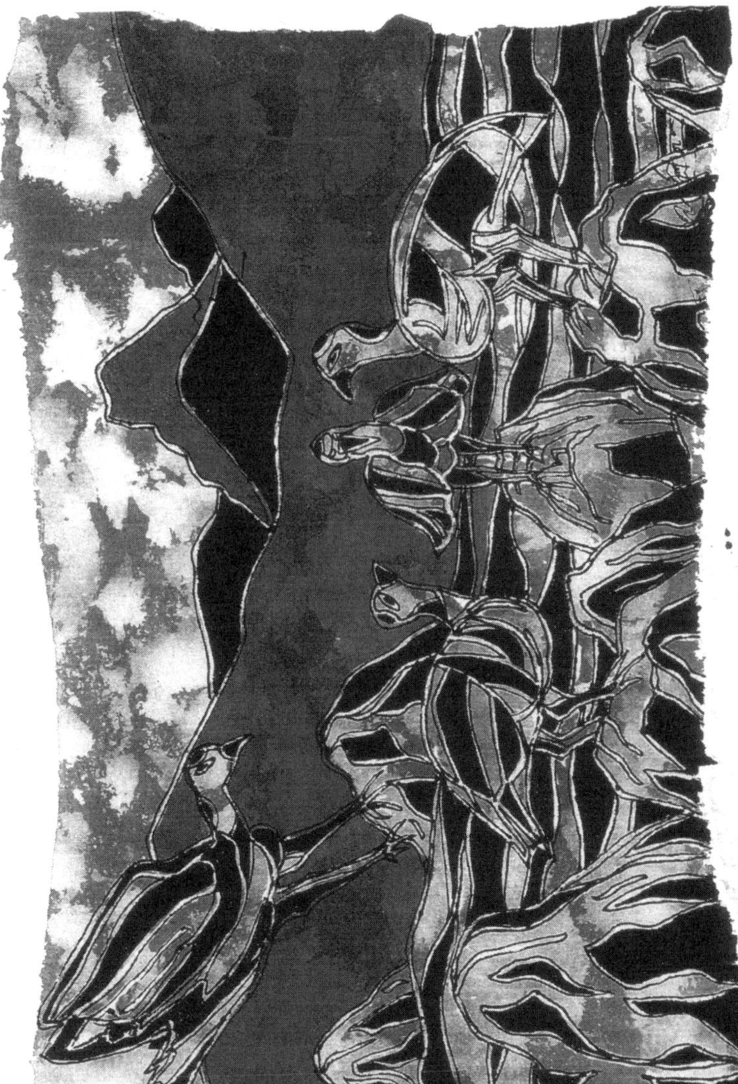

The Girl at the Train Station

THERE'S ALWAYS a strange atmosphere of travel in train stations, an undetermined sensation of instability, of aimless routes. Freight cars slowly cross the yards and their closed compartments, made of rotted wood covered with a strange rust, leave behind at the edge of the tracks the smell of certain imaginary cargoes. There in the station old corners survive the decades: a ticket booth with greenish windows and modernist details within which nestle lost cats, rats and migratory birds. An abandoned wing of the station smells like oil, and in the penumbra of late afternoon the penetrating wind of diesel fuel penetrates the walls. A girl leaps over the coupling of a train carrying immense petroleum pipes and dirties her tennis shoes with grease, while the locomotive's whistle suddenly makes her jump over the rails.

The sky is a deep blue. In old abandoned cars next to immense containers that pass the days in the rain live people who are as well abandoned. A man closes a torn dirty curtain and takes out a bowl of scraps so that a cat with remote Siamese lineage can eat, its tail raised and gaze fierce. A few pot-bellied children run among the improvised habitations, coming and going beneath the locomotive's metal wheels capable of crushing iron bars and prehistoric stones.

At the end of the year in the lands of the northern hemisphere, the slanting setting sun incisively cuts through the atmosphere, emitting an intense orange light charged with nostalgia. It is a most loving sun, a sun that resuscitates strange emotions in the misled travelers, a sun that changes the face of things and transmutes them thanks to the strange alchemy of imaginary, eternal objects, where the life that thousands, millions of world travelers have passed through is concentrated. Behind the station, caressed as well by the nostalgic color of the autumn sun, can be seen several old mansions now fallen into disrepair. Perhaps in another time, in this city or this village, the houses bordering the train station were animated by the intense life of commerce and vice. Now in the empty rooms are seen slashed paintings, the colors made uniform by the mold and dim light. In the empty stores where today only mangy dogs live there were in other times gambling parlors, places of lively festivities for motorists and merchants. Now those houses look like the rotted teeth of an antediluvian animal and the streets, empty and sad, only stir to locomotive whistles, the desperate hissing of steam, the sharp screech of couplings and wheels.

Thus is every train station in every town in the world. But there sitting on a rusty cart the chosen girl drinks tequila, while next to her some old women look at her long hair, her bulky blue and yellow striped wool sweater, her scarf, her jeans and her tennis shoes stained by grease. The light becomes clearer and the conjunction of tubes, cylinders, cones, hangars, stores, rails, rickety wood and relegated cars takes on the tonalities of a future painting situated in the terrain of an adventurous past. The girl leans against the darkened walls and has pulled her hair back so she can look with her round eyeglasses at the corrals where, separated by barbed wire fences, several cows and bulls sleep or graze in the cloudless space. The cold wind from the volcanoes gathers in intensity over the train station, stirring curtains, raising dust, carrying from one corner to another the smell of saw dust and oil, grease and rotted wood.

Fat men in tee-shirts and baseball caps with rough and calloused hands move the rails or get ready to open the water spigot to fill some locomotive. A beggar digs through trash cans; a few Indians carry chickens in sacks or wooden crates. The station platforms fill with people. The train with the oil pipes slowly leaves and is lost in the distant desert of the high mountains adorned with pines and savage snowy winds. Later the train arrives and stops so passengers can get off and board. There the black-haired girl will agilely jump on and be seen running down a car full of people that carry in their bodies the profound smell of a nation, that inconfutable, loving smell of the centuries. Farther on, almost at the end of the train, the girl from the station will lean back against an upholstered seat and take another sip of tequila. The train pulls out and the conductors in torn uniforms and old hats take the tickets. When night falls, the train will whistle through the mountain range and the cold wind will pass down the aisles. A few volatile seeds will cover the hair of the girl who throws her legs over the seat in front of her; perhaps thinking of someone like herself, she dreams of meeting by chance another being on a street corner, in a cafeteria, in the next seat on an airplane, in a hotel room, at a bus station, in a park or next to an abandoned passenger car full of scattered voices. A shadow will then fall from the high mountains and settle beside her so it can smell her scent and feel her breath: a presence, the heat of a mysterious occult being that reveals neither identity nor name. It will only be the vestige, the solid rustic mass of what some call love and others associate with death.

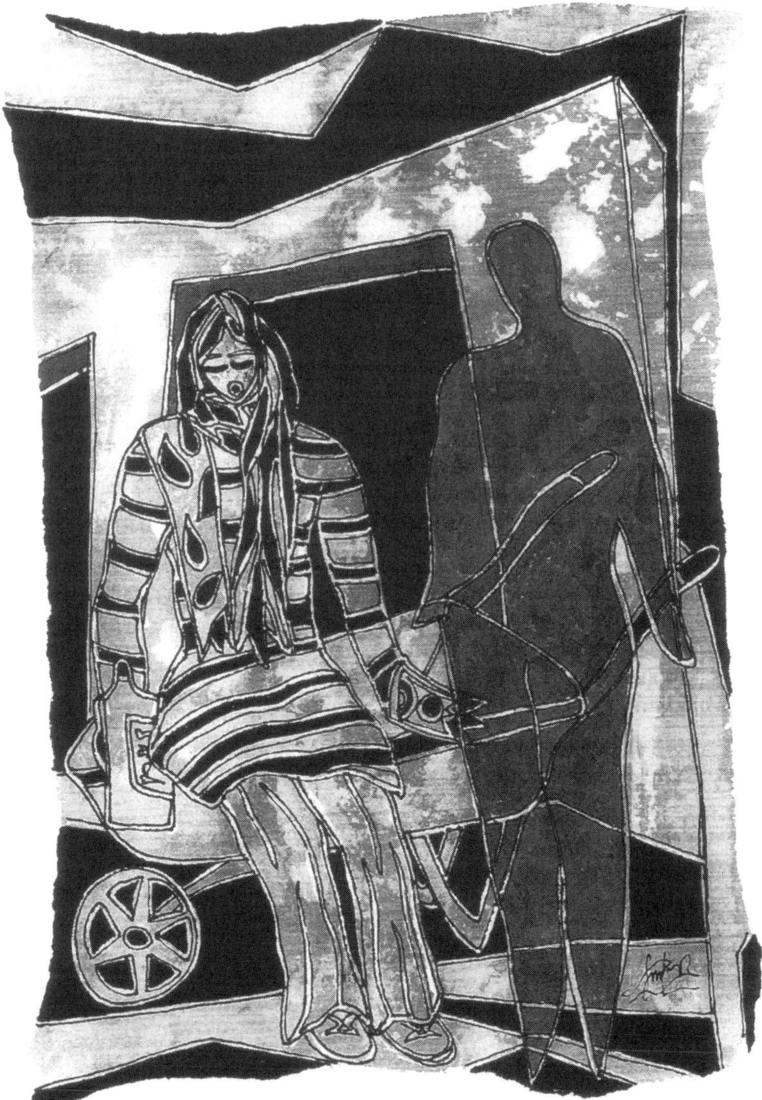

Dream of the Sewers

I HEAR A CAVERNOUS VOICE, as if from the netherworld, beside me. A mustached man getting on in years holds out his hand, chewing on a few incomprehensible words, the password of some secret brotherhood of the living. He has no legs, but two stumps covered by a blue cloth torn by endless crawling. Nor does he have a left hand. A bald dislocated appendage ends in four agile fingers. He speaks, thinks and looks about hoping for a conversation, a minimal gaze that would confirm for him his existence. Horrified, he turns his gaze to a group of boys bundling old newspapers and a fat smiling man with a food stand.

The horrible creature, wearing a green military shirt, puts distance between us and drags himself along the Calle Donato Guerra, pushing aside the garbage and scaring off a few dogs that come up to sniff him. I look at my feet and my hands, and following his steps I have the sensation that my legs have been grafted from another being, another body, another strange creature. I follow his anguished though able

111

steps, the imaginary steps of nonexistent legs; I observe the remains of the muscled hand that pushes with difficulty upon the cobblestones and dirty dust and I go after him.

The man pants and looks at me again, hurrying his steps, and powerful drops of viscous sweat—as if composed of smoke, smog, salt, earth—roll from his forehead. He jumps the curb and crosses the street between broken down vehicles missing parts and the legs of hurrying people: here a pregnant woman in a stifling overcoat, there a slow old gray-haired man with a cane half out of breath, here a vagabond and there a Lolita. The man tries to disappear among those legs from my ever more penetrating gaze.

"Where are you going?" I shout.

The man speeds up and already quite a bit ahead of me manages to answer, his eyes shining with a lucid and febrile innocence. "To work. I work, too."

The bald and muscled hand displays the iron tendons and cartilage that have supported him throughout his existence. "What do you want?" he adds.

"Nothing, I just want to look at you. I can't understand how you manage to survive."

People pass by without noticing that man who like a decrepit old iguana crawls over the sands of a hot, monotonous desert. Their pallid and inexpressive faces rest upon bodies even more pallid and dead. The wind paints a flash of sun and in the distance, in the late afternoon, the old buildings on Reforma turn into gigantic coals of solid firewood. Rare lost birds cross the dirty sky blazing in disgust. A deafening sound filters through the cracks and crevices of the street and mixes in the night of the sewers, inhabited by undiscovered beings.

112

"Where do you live, man, where do you live?"

"In the sewers," he answers me.

I think about his tired breath and the effort it takes to lift the heavy, gigantic manhole covers. I can imagine him creeping through the humid, dark, sinister tunnels populated by nightwalkers and forgotten beings. I see his heart beating in a corner while an unexpected odor of filthy water overflows the subterranean sidewalks, leaving a scummy residue where he sleeps.

"Don't ask me any more questions, I live, that's all, leave me alone...One has to live and I live."

I see him inhabiting a universe of tubes and hatches beaten by the sound of the waves of shit. I feel him sleeping in some forgotten recess below ground, next to a sepulchral temple silently destroyed by the public works. I hear him meekly panting at midnight, lulled by the oceanic sound of his shadow. Rats are his friends. Immense overfed rats which dominate the intricate labyrinth of the sewers; not the labyrinth of dreams, but the labyrinth of useless horrors.

While the nocturnal streets delude themselves with stoplights, with lights coming from rooms inhabited by lovers, young gay men, desirous women; while the sound of a few vehicles comes around the corner and a scream is lost in the neighborhood, soon destroyed like the voice of a thousand phantoms, this creature creeps silently amid the shit and piss. He discovers new marvelous recesses in the intersection of two gigantic conduits. He screams and takes comfort hearing his echo. He gathers his force and climbs a wall overlooking the invisible dregs. His wet clothing has superimposed itself into a tactile skin. His feline eyes shine and cast their luminosity over the moldy walls dressed in lichens. That creature finally falls exhausted and lies trapped in the nets of the sounds surrounding him, while in the surface world watchful beings hurry to sink naked in the inevitable, horrid, shiny, unnecessary tunnels of their dreams.

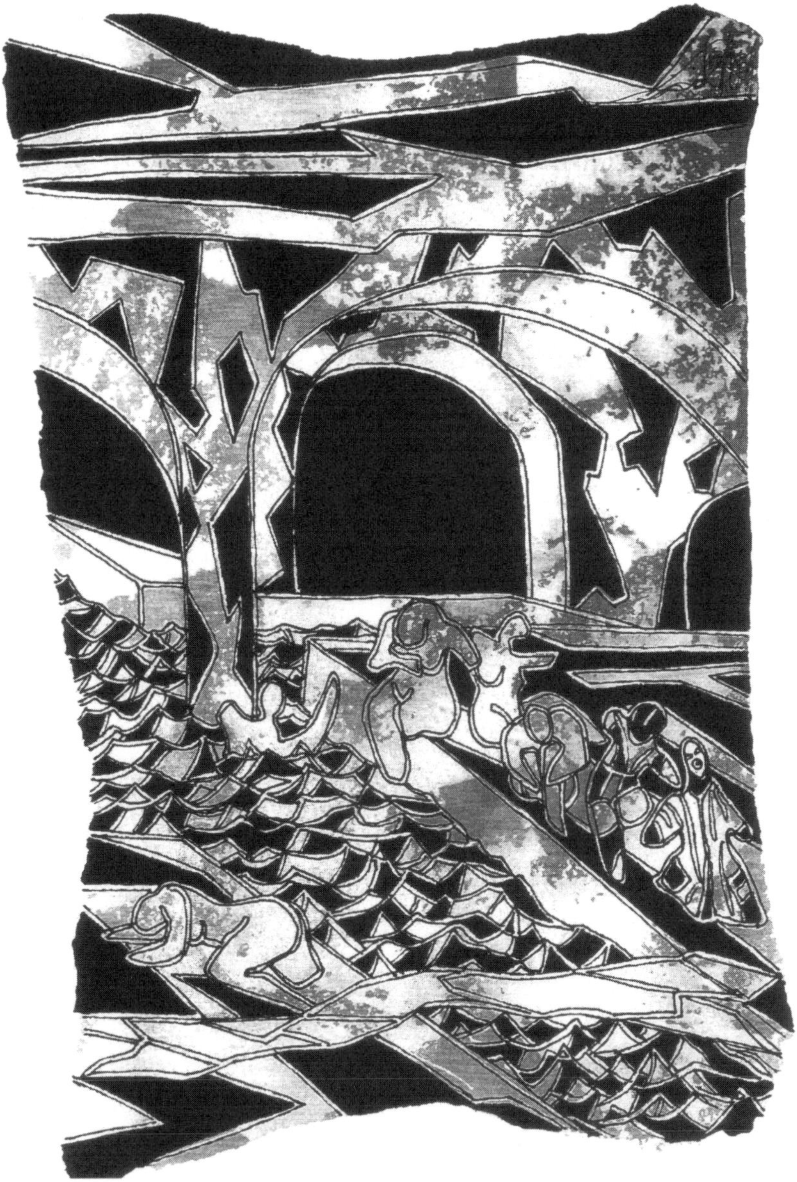

Roses for a City in Ruins

NEXT TO THE BAGS of garbage set out on
Amsterdam Avenue thrive the nocturnal scavengers.
Voracious as ants, they carry off the detritus, they se-
lect their booty and finally analyze with their shining
eyes the rescued objects. Gray beings, some of them
wear dirty torn clothing. But there's one man I find
amazing: he wears a tie and broad-brimmed hat like
they did during the period of Porfirio Rovirosa. Is he
by chance a poet? Many years have passed since
Mexico's boom times; at the beginning of the new
millenium the middle-class wanders the streets like
destitute drunks did in other times. The rich have become richer and the poor poorer. Laborers and lower-
class men who frequent only *pulquerías* and beer halls
manage to survive thanks to the wisdom of those who
have always been on the edge of nothingness. They
look with disdain at their new members from the
middle-class who now, in 2002, struggle to displace
them from their fortune. The man wears an old Pierre
Cardin necktie and in a pocket of his worn-out trench

coat is seen the cover of a book by Goethe. A sparse white beard gives a Biblical air to this character on Amsterdam Avenue. Many of the old mansions that during previous years shone in their art-nouveau style have been replaced by buildings with high glass walls. When they leave their offices, government officials are guarded in trucks with tinted windows. The situation has become so difficult that the lynch mobs don't act with political motives, but out of the need to strip their victims of valuable objects. Poets, who used to enjoy great power, are now condemned to survive by searching through the garbage for discarded things. Insurgentes Avenue is an immense solitary freeway covered by garbage and dust. Automobiles have disappeared and the potentates are transported in carts pulled by beasts. Around them march soldiers with rifles. From the corners the glassy gaze of the miserable penetrates the sides of those new vehicles.

It is night. I haven't been back to Mexico City for many years. I wanted to come, before dying, to retrace my steps over the Amsterdam Avenue where I used to ride my bicycle. A few buildings are covered by dried moss and little lizards rapidly run among the stones. I look for my friend's house, but it has been destroyed and in its place is an empty lot where greasy men beat on iron sheets. At night the whirlwinds become stronger. Smog has disappeared, but a mass of dust has inundated the city and people war face masks. Hordes of children wander the avenues letting out indescribable moans. Later, near the Parque de Mexico, I see the beggar take out the book by Goethe. He reads aloud incomprehensible phrases in German. The trees are dried and shriveled and the same purple crepuscular wind that moves the fallen leaves of Amsterdam

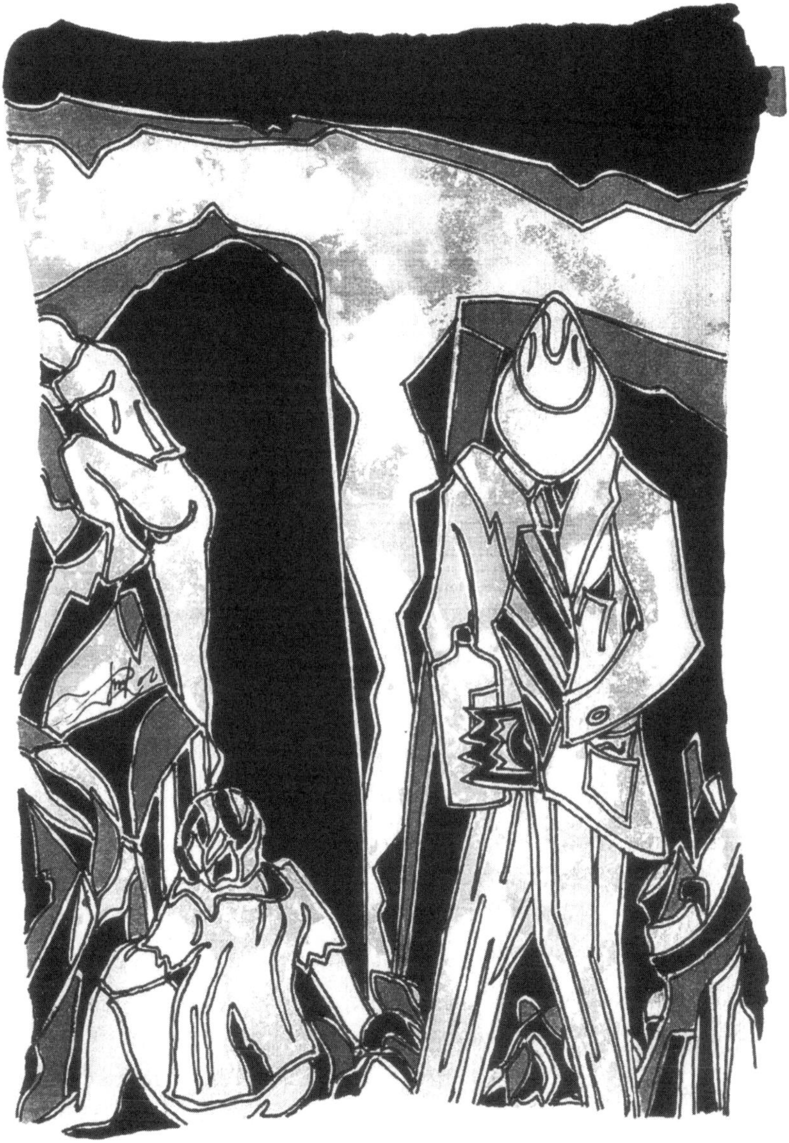

Avenue attacks the park's shriveled grass. The canals are full of dead leaves, the fountain site covered by orange lichens.

In the distance the howl of hungry coyotes sounds. Music from a piano emerges from an old apartment building and wafts down to the park where I have come to record my youth and my loves. The man in the necktie holds out his hand and offers me his green liquor bottle. I grab it and drink the crystalline water it contains. Later I throw myself down on the dry earth to rest. Three tears escape slowly from my eyes filled with nostalgia. I cry for an irretrievable past, for the flowers from years gone by, for the smog that despite everything else was less arid than the wind of this catastrophe. From a balcony a beautiful girl, her hair loose and flowing, casts me a smile. She goes back into her room illuminated by a greenish light and softly begins playing a piano melody.

III

STENDHAL AND FLAUBERT
IN THE STOMACH

Tunnels

WE WELCOME with pleasure the voices that suddenly surge from the past and lodge in our quarters. For some five years the Paris subway brought me on its journey the figure of an elegant young classical flutist who would station himself at an intersection of the metro Chatelet's tunnels to play incredible melodies. Or the figure of that beautiful Caribbean mulatta accompanied by the handsome Antillean band. Or the image of that beautiful and diminutive Bolivian dressed in blue jeans and a native shirt, with long hair and smooth skin, playing a *queña* along with a band of her compatriots.

The melody of the *zampoñas* flies through time and space here to me...

Let's recall the long corridors of the metro station Nation, trying to elude the gendarmes. Let's walk along the outside platforms of the station Bastille, reading a newspaper that discusses young Portuguese captains or war in Africa. A delicious weave of tunnels, the warp and woof of the length, width and depth of Paris. A thousand stations, a thousand platforms, blurry figures, illusions, a song, that poem, a book, an overcoat, the blackness, the night, the cold. Ice. All this has thrust itself today into my room. I breathe in the accumulations of some afternoon.

I emerge from the tunnel of the subterranean floors of the Bazar Hotel de Ville and afterwards lose myself in the streets of Le Marais dreaming of a future time, corridors unknown and unimagined, where I now carry my body and the illusions that continue to live on renewed within it. I hear the rain on the September platforms. How I wish sometimes I might be able to burrow like a mole through this tropical land and construct my tunnel to your beloved streets.

I would like to suddenly appear on those corners where I would steal *Le Monde* or *L'Express* when I had no money and sit at some bistro having an afternoon coffee, lodged in the intemporality of exile, in the inspaciality of travel. To visit the strange countries whose innumerable representatives wander next to me or play pinball in the corners of time. To suddenly appear in Morocco or in Tunis, in Tozeur, in the land of Zouzi el-Chebbi.

If the world were only a subway and we ticketless passengers traveling through the valleys and most distant steppes. To find myself here on the corner and appear later standing on a wharf in Java or Melbourne. To alight in Bombay and take off for New York. To retire and rest in Cartagena. To look closely at the location of that aquamarine city, the umbilicus of the tropics, the station where the best they can do is hope for the Abominable Snowman.

I raise my hand here in the room and there appears a silk scarf. I direct my gaze toward the ceiling and see the frescos of the Sistine Chapel or Saint-Savain. I close my eyes and I'm at a fiesta at the Wagram Hall, where Brando and Schneider danced.

I open my mouth and drops of some liquor I haven't tasted fall from it: a kiss I don't understand. I open the drawers of my dresser and there shine crystals, old Tarot cards, letters from friends, a rabbit's foot. Around me shine masks, bottles, umbrellas, scarves, coats, black leather jackets, blankets, purple cushions, little patent leather shoes, a kaleidoscope, the skull of the night, the star of the south, a broken compass. I remove the books and open the door to the perfect, silent, clean library in a recess of Tours and, flying through the air I find an old woman who knew Leon Bloy that guides me through the wide corridors formed by the bookshelves: I wouldn't have time to look at its million books, I could die there searching for and never finding the imaginary book I am unable to write.

I open the window and a December snow storm blows in and I see the Mexican streets and the Plaza Rio de Janeiro turned completely white, the Latin American Tower in Mexico City a gigantic snowman.

Inside the little bottle of correcting fluid lies a narcotic. The Kores corrigible paper has sticky acids. The golden watch my father gave me as a gift doesn't tell time: it speaks of interstellar space and counts unknown stars. The typewriter speaks. Two wooden monks look at me from the window sill and from the center of a beautiful clay candelabrum a candle illuminates the darkness. It's a tunnel. Everything has been revoked. Witches fly in my room. The music of jazz players in Montmartre or the congos of Cerete reach all the way here.

127

Dreams like a white silk curtain. Words like marihuana leaves. Night like living inside a bottle of wine.

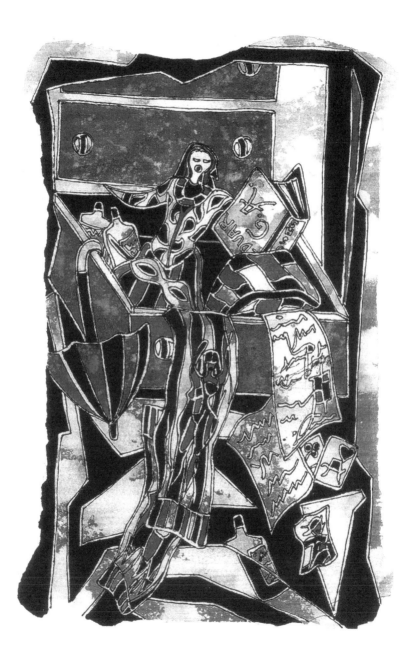

A Damned Little Guide to Paris

A DELIRIOUS CONCENTRIC weave begins to take form between the underground and the air in the imaginary city of Paris. Pressed together in the darkness, thousands of skulls and skeletons fill the labyrinth of catacombs, the center of a cavernous rite visited especially by fictional beings. On one side of the underbelly of the city extend those mysterious *égouts*, the sewers, almost paradisiacal to the precursors of the "underground." Huge rodents, putrid waters, canals and musty corridors serve as scenery for the roughest adventures: forgotten beings with a deathly pallor, wise beggars, escaped prisoners and a network of mournful employees travel in little boats over the blackened waters. From up above experts throw enormous balls of some unknown material, charged with dislodging potential reefs and clearing the way for the waters. One can imagine the clamor of the enormous sphere when it reaches maximum velocity, the devastation it leaves behind before it's captured again in another corner of the city. In this intricate world everything is possible, from love to death, from brotherhood to hermeticism. Some being from beyond the tomb will have chosen a corner there, fleeing from the swarming civilization sprawled upon the Seine's old riverbanks; already friend to the enormous predators descending from those who once populated the market of Les Halles, he will converse with them and share their solitude, their voices echoing through the corridors of that parallel world, the threatening scream of those pests with wet leathery skin.

Perfect settings for some damned novel or a few brief histories with heroes from hell, the catacombs and the *égouts* (sewers, conduits, drains, culverts, according to the dictionary) belong to the city's most aristocrat class, and their archeology and history can unchain fierce thoughts: there would be concentrated the network of brotherhoods rebelling against the "progress" of the surface; in the subterranean no-city one could develop the gears, the machinery of an improbable phalanstery. From the catacombs and sewers will emerge those charged with repopulating a surface exhausted by war. The millennium will not have made an impression on them, accompanied as they are by the detritus, the vestiges, the garbage of civilization. Amid the rust, the dust and the musty earth of this secret Paris will accumulate indecipherable layers of keys in different forms, designs and sizes, and with them the doors of light will be opened.

The subway is something else entirely. Already a hundred years old and consecrated by use, this other labyrinthine urb guards in its breast the massacre of the metro Charonne and a chorus of those who have committed suicide. From among the thousands of millions of travelers could be found material for an international museum of gestures of solitude: the lost gazes of widows, orphans, abandoned women, recently freed prisoners, exiles, lovers on the edge of desperation, solitary people driven mad by the absence of another's body, recently court-martialed soldiers, ambitious provincial youths (with the look of a Rastignac or Rubempre), adventurers from exotic Conradian countries.

Amid the sound of the wheels on the rails, the shaking of old wood, the explosion of compressed air, the play of the pistons, each person descending toward the underground will confront himself or herself in the mirror. Even the blind know that there the gaze reigns, whether fleeting, direct, mad, glassy, teary, tame, aggressive. Bells, sirens, people walking and running, sweat, briefcases, shined shoes, jackets from the flea market, black and yellow and white men, pygmies, Incas, bags, coins, cameos, necklaces, diadems, gold and emerald earrings, filth, lips painted like a vamp, the laugh of a *loubard,* the metro would be a delicacy for the lover of catalogues, for an observer like Georges Pérec, ready to write a book of instructions on subterranean life. The best and most difficult list to develop would be that of the imagination. What do they think, what have they thought, those hundred thousand million beings stopped in that detained time of interurban travel, how many ideas or images will have surged there and stay impregnated in the oval tunnel, mixed in with the delicious vintage smell of the stations?

But beyond the hundred sorts of publicity posters, beyond the *cour de miracles* peopled by singers from Madagascar or Port-au-Prince, flutists from La Paz or tambourine players from Senegal, the most valid

133

and important voice of this city in movement is that of the suicidal, who with their atrocious acts try to shake awake the anesthetized. The arrival of the ambulances, the running nurses and then the extraction of the broken body from the oily gravel leaves a bitter taste in the mouths of those who continue on their way toward every point of the compass. He who commits suicide in the metro is one possessed by the neighboring catacombs or the sinister sewers. By a subterfuge of osmosis, the subway's suicidal is called to his true terrain; in his grave he will be lulled by the waters, the cars, the dust, the cellar gazes.

Walter Benjamin—the melancholic *confrère* of exile who with Roth, Tsvetaieva and Beckett is part of the unending gallery of foreigners who have lived in Paris—refers in his text, "Paris, Capital of the Nineteenth Century," to the formation of a curious labyrinth of trade in the surface city. Speaking of the *magasins de nouveautés*, predecessors of the large department stores, he discusses the genealogy of the underside of the city. With the advent of textiles, the construction of iron and glass is developed and reaches its peak in the middle of the nineteenth century. The warehouse, the store, the walkway, the gallery will constitute in a certain form the essence of the modern city. Windows filled with merchandise and boulevards full of anxious crowds will create the pedestrian, the *flâneur*, the new version of the *promeneur.* The latter is an emanation of observable nature, while the former emanates from the street. Thus as the lost gaze is the lasso of the subterranean traveler, the curious gaze will end up becoming the instrument of the urban pedestrian. The dandy dresses up so he will be seen along the boulevard, while the poor man will have access to

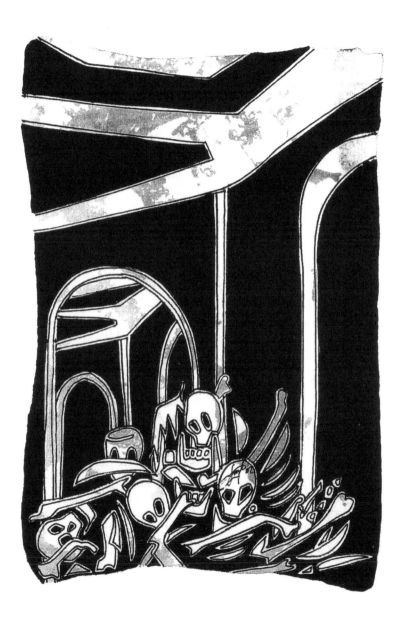

the spectacles of store windows and nourish his penury from outside. Telescopes, suits, hunting rifles, accessories for orthopedists, paintings, colorful fish, toy soldiers, and flowers are some of the merchandise that give a reason for being to the network of backstreets.

Now let us discuss the bistro, the absolute king of Paris, the vendor of the most exquisite merchandise: alcohol and coffee, without which many would venture to say the splendor of Paris is not possible. They exist everywhere in the world, but only in that city do they accomplish their true function. On every block there are a number of these locations, with their own regular clientele who respect the hours of the establishment. Let's recall those alcoholic owners with the reddened noses, dominated by the imposing matron who carefully observes the movements of the noisy clientele while she pours beers or prepares an espresso, of the uniformed worker who leaves the shop and arrives to his bistro on the rue Jean-Pierre Timbaud or the enfeebled Cortazarian piano player who drinks and hears his past at a table on the rue des Solitaires. The pinball players swimming in their black leather jackets, the pallid poet who speaks of the centuries amid the smoke from his Gitane or Gauloise, the old man who stops a moment with a baguette under his arm while he drinks his first calvados. Images for a strange guide of exoticism. Someone once said that the great misfortune of native Parisians is that they will never be able to say happily, "I'm going to visit Paris." It's obvious that a concierge or a *clochard,* an ill-humored shopkeeper on the corner or an old prostitute nostalgic for Frehel or Damia is no big deal to a native of Paris. For the visitor, on the other hand, they will serve to begin their ethnological catalogue of exoticism. The Paris bistro, the great King, the true sovereign of the labyrinth, the maestro, is for the errant intellectual as surprising as an Amazonian village where aborigines chew leaves and eat mojojoy worms at twilight. For this reason, Julio Cortazar's *Hopscotch* is the bible for a generation of Latin Americans who searched during the '70s for that imaginary Paris of the surrealists, and were left seduced by its streets and the nostalgia of something absent, immersed in the "exotic."

We still have to climb up to the garrets, the other key strand in this city's weave, as important as Benjamin's galleries and landscapes. This is a city above the city, full of cries, memories, happiness and sex. First constructed for servants, they were converted into the residences of students, foreigners, lost people, young painters, ambitious musicians, dealers of the latest drugs, pornographers and nymph hunters. One gets to them by poorly lit dusty service staircases, on the margins, going against the current. Salinger and Cameron's beautiful book of photography, *Au-dessus de Paris,* though seemingly dedicated to looking at the city from above, would be a great homage to garrets. They appear in the foreground, reflecting the June light between chimneys and slanted roofs. Perhaps there the young enamored Japanese man devoured his lover bit by bit, savoring her muscles, her neck, her angelic fingers. There great works of contemporary literature were written and a notable number of lovers of the Bohemian underground emerged. Diminutive cubicles where people are crowded together, long dusty corridors leading to communal bathrooms, water faucets in the corners of this strange boulevard. Doves hunted for food, a city of roofs, feline and promiscuous, still deserving the homage of joyful pariahs. The contemporary version of the medieval road taken by vagabonds, where the saltimbanco and his partner the harlequin, the mountebank, the knave forge their deeds.

Tunnels, concavities, spiral staircases, rolling carpets, cobblestone streets, walkways, flea markets, bistros, great warehouses, sidewalks, parks, churches, ruins. How many thousands of words are needed to name one of the most passionate adventures in civilization and, of course, barbarity?

Stendhal and Flaubert in the Stomach

A BOOK CAN BE converted into a character or a passage of time that carries us to unexpected and absurd locations. Such is the tragic story of *Madame Bovary, Red and Black* and *The Charterhouse of Parma* which I bought in a Stockholm bookstore. I began reading them in a restaurant where I washed dishes, helped out by water hoses and the collaboration of two rubicund young Polish women who cursed Gierek and anointed themselves with entire bottles of French perfume. I would sit down in my dirty white apron spattered with filth and take from my bag *Red and Black* and *The Charterhouse of Parma*, at that time my only salvation against boredom. My Turkish companions, an older couple who treated me like an unfortunate but beloved son and a young Westernized Yugoslav who worked every summer in the capitalist inferno of Sweden to help out his family in the Socialist paradise, were impressed to see me sitting there reading books or next to the dishwasher, leaning against the chrome bars holding in one hand the tome and in the other a hose that sprayed an implacable stream of water against the plates. It didn't take me long to notice their attention. Unfortunately for them, I had devoured the two volumes and would soon leave, frustrating any designs they had.

I then traveled to Paris with the Garnier edition of *Madame Bovary*, ready to devour the book. It was a delicious, insomniac week, one of those lapses in life caressed by unforgettable reading. I read in the cafés of the Arab neighborhood of Belleville, warmed by a couple beers and listening to the jukebox music in the background, letting myself be dazzled by the colored lights shining through the screen where sensual women from Kabylia or Tozeur performed Arabic dances. Possessed by history, steered on by it, I marked many points and admirable thoughts and underlined special passages on the satiny paper of that beloved edition. The scene when they bestow a decoration upon a humble old woman, Rodolphe's cape, the confetti thrown from the carriage in which Emma and Leon give themselves over to each other, Rodolphe's walk through the gentle grounds of the region, the unsuccessful operation on the writhing man prodded on by Homais and so many other stories contained in the novel made me a solid mass at one with the book, which once finished on a star-filled night peopled by Arabs and hawkers out of some scene from *Salambo* sat on the bookshelf until one terrible day.

That was when I had to sell the books to eat. An impossible moment had arrived. The imposing need to sell them was as certain as an Arab scimitar. Those books that inhabited and filled years and months and whose writing was as familiar and dear to me as no other, had withstood attack for several months, but it was no longer possible to distance them from the daily vicissitudes of their owner, this writer.

I can't forget the day I picked them up because they were sellable. The only thing I had left were those editions, almost pocketbooks, for which the vendors at Gibert gave a few devalued francs. I went up the Boulevard Saint Michel with them in a grocery bag, entered the ground floor, and took an elevator to the top floor.

There were two buyers there, a monumental and flaccid albino with Norman features and a purple-lipped dry old maid, whose gaze of a frustrated hydra fell over the books with the most formidable speed.

Their appraisal could not be appealed, like my destiny. They knew how to reject you with a sole glance, allowing no reclamation, or they would offer laughable prices for good and sometimes new editions. We assiduous clients of the top floor belonged to a quite noble brotherhood, although we chewed on our unfortunate pride with the sweet syrup of uncomprehending genius. We stood in line hiding our gazes from each other, scrutinizing with our imposed indifference the treasures of the other and we lamented in solidarity when some obscure poet from the suburbs, squalid as a street corner cur, had to go away with his bag full of scorned books, sadly imagining his luckless future or plotting secret actions that struck with the sword of deferred glory at such an infamous destiny.

For the edition of *Madame Bovary*, bound and in good condition, they gave me eight francs, which was a fortune. For Stendhal's *The Charterhouse of Parma* and *Red and Black* eight and five francs respectively, which made another thirteen. With my twenty-one francs from the quick and successful trans-

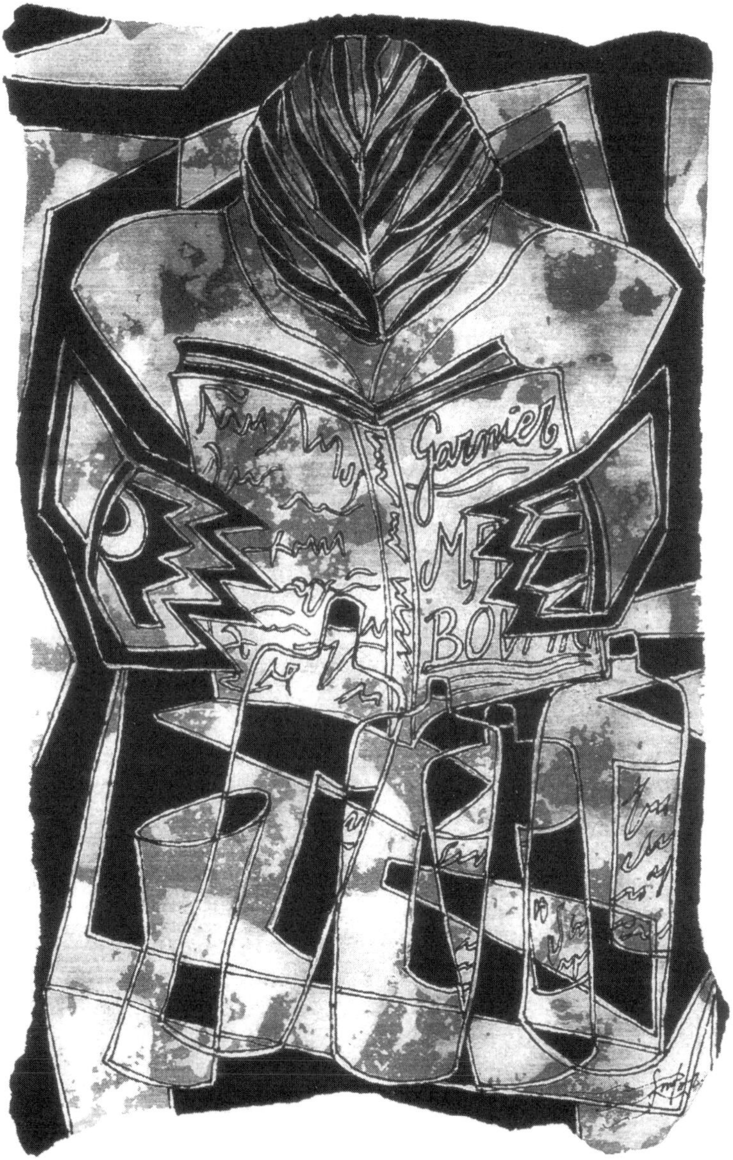
Garnier

action I was able to eat some cous-cous and drink a beer in a fly-filled North African restaurant and with what was left over I bought a few metro tickets, although one should realize it wasn't difficult to sneak for free under the metal turn-styles and then avoid the police.

I don't know the destiny of those three precious books I so loved and vilely betrayed, during one of those inscrutable moments of life when aesthetic principles are dominated by gastric juices and intestinal cramps. I would have liked to know who was fortunate enough to buy them for triple the price, who enjoyed them and where.

Later I searched for them on the bookstore's shelves with the intention of rescuing them, because I was once again rich and feeling like a character out of a Biblical story. Like those mythical princesses that in the secret of their misfortune decide to place their most luxurious possessions in a chest, abandoned to the chance of rivers and seas, I left mine to the chance of an unsuspected passage through time. Now, several years later, I still haven't lost hope of rescuing them and placing them upon the altar they deserve, with the most frugal and pure care and indulgence.

Secret Ceremony

PIERRE GOLDMAN DID what Sartre couldn't: commit armed robbery and then read Hegel. This most brilliant and emotional youth of the generation of May 1968 was a prudent, timid and scornful intellectual, but brave in debate when necessary. During those events that so marked our century, he participated in a movement called the Katangese, composed of people who detested ideological straight-jackets and seized any opportunity to create disorder, erect barricades and stir madness, which the orthodox bureaucrats would later strangle with weak, tired Marxist-Evangelical supplications.

Deceived and enraged he decided like the gentle Debray to try his luck in the Latin American mountains, an experience which ended so fucked up that the only thing left for him to do was visit the Bogotá bordellos, where he could say "their pussies were like suction cups." And he came back a lover of Caribbean music. After returning to Paris, loathed by all the wimps who had installed themselves in the bureaucratic posts and pedestals of the Central Committee, he decided to become a bandit, trying to earn the profound respect of the Antillean blacks he hung out with. He first tried to rob the psychoanalyst Jacques Lacan, but with no success: in his book *Obscure Memories of a Polish Jew Born in France*, he relates how he watched Lacan coming down the steps of his office building and how some strange force of compassion for this old man prevented him from committing sacrilege. He later successfully robbed warehouses, safes and business offices, like some reincarnation of the scoundrel and poet François Villon. With the money he got he cut his hair in the best salons on the Champs-Élysées, bought elegant suits and drank the most exquisite liquors, until the day when accused by some unnamed informant, an individual who never wanted to denounce him, he was arrested and accused of the homicide of two humble pharmacists on the Boulevard Richard Lenoir.

The trial was quite well publicized and among those attending were Simone Signoret and Yves Montand, as well as comrades from his own generation, who without sufficient evidence couldn't prevent him from being sentenced to life imprisonment. As was said of Bloy, "The democratic institution of the jury, in virtue of which a superior man is put at the mercy of twelve clowns created to serve on it, is so perfect that the unfortunate one cannot challenge his judges... Moreover, from the first day on, the jury demonstrated a ferocious, almost open, hatred toward him. They were shopkeepers, and they were trying to judge a poet." For a collective crime, the French establishment managed to sentence to life in prison the generation of May Goldman incarnated.

In prison Pierre Goldman, who had passively observed the verdict and disdained any movement created to aid him, submerged himself in a muteness broken only by an Antillean woman he was in love with who awaited him to marry.

He decided then to pen one of the most brilliant essays ever conceived, written with a certain kind of innocence. An adventure novel in the manner of *A Long Day's Journey into Night,* where he relates his childhood, his adolescence, May '68, his travels through the world, his frustrations; a treaty on penal and ballistic law, a kind of psychological study of victims and accusers, a police story, feverish theoretical prose. Its title: *Souvenirs obscurs d'un juif polonais né en France.*

The verdict's appeal moved the entire country. Everyday on the front page came news about the appeal, which resulted in his acquittal and a reduced sentence he finished months later. When he got out of prison he became director of a famous literary collection, a contributor to *Les Temps Modernes*, and an occasional contributor to *Libération,* the newspaper founded by the cross-eyed philosopher.

The right-wing, or the police, which is the same thing, didn't forgive Goldman for living with a black Antillean woman, his Latin American friendships, his skill at playing the congas, his bohemian life in Chapelle des Lombards and his splendid, although discrete, literary career marked by his new novel.

One afternoon in September 1979, a bullet struck him down in a little park in the thirteenth arrondissement. Hours later would be born his first son, Manuel, the dream of his life: the union of Jew and Black. Those two novelistic events would join

148

for the first time a generation already forty years old who desired to settle accounts with their professional disillusionment.

It was precisely at his burial that I accomplished a life-long dream with two young Jewish friends Manolo and Heny: seeing Sartre. We ended up meeting near the rear wall of Père Lachaise, the cemetery where Oscar Wilde is buried and where Rastignac, at the end of *Père Goriot* shouts at Paris, "Between us two, henceforth!"

We had the privilege of attending the private ceremony in company of special guests such as André Glucksman, Bernard-Henri Lévy, Régis Debray, Simone Signoret, Yves Montand and many other characters from the press and the intellectual world who looked at each other out of the corner of their eyes with the hatred of old repressed rivalries. Like stone guests, we attended the sorrow of a generation that understood the end of its youth and the arrival of the future, that celebrated the burial of a heroic epoch. In a certain way they were burying Marxism-Leninism to the sound of the congas of Azuquita, a Panamanian salsa player whose group Goldman used to sit in with.

Suddenly a beat-up dusty blue Renault cut short the intimate ceremony, slowly and strangely heading toward the temporary tomb. We wondered what sacred cow had just arrived. A trembling wrinkled hand emerged from the car, and then, held up almost entirely by the stiff and erect Simone de Beauvoir and a friend, emerged Sartre, who couldn't shut his open and painfully blubbering lips. Shuffling along in short steps, bent over, a decrepit Jean-Paul Sartre was there among us. He walked a bit toward the tomb until he fainted from emotion or fatigue; a famous photo shows him seated on a bench, beside a mausoleum that foretells his death.

We left Père Lachaise shortly afterwards. The children of Goldman, the autonomous anarchists of the atomic era, started to riot on the Boulevard Belleville, just like during the good old days of May when Goldman was a celebrated Katangese. Stones flew at cars and at the police, people ran through the packed streets of the Arab quarter, alarms sounded and ambulances arrived to rescue the wounded. The secret fury of a rebel with a cause.

Soaked by the rain, Manolo, Heny and I finished our espressos and contemplated the spectacle, aware we could never forget Sartre and would stay forever joined in that recollection that still remains in my memory.

At the burial of a Polish Jew born in France, in the company of a Jewish woman from Argentina and a Jewish man from Colombia, I understood that life always offers great emotion and that illusion has yet to be lost in the dark penumbra of a collapsed and rusty tunnel, yet to be struck down by the bullets of furious political disenchantment.

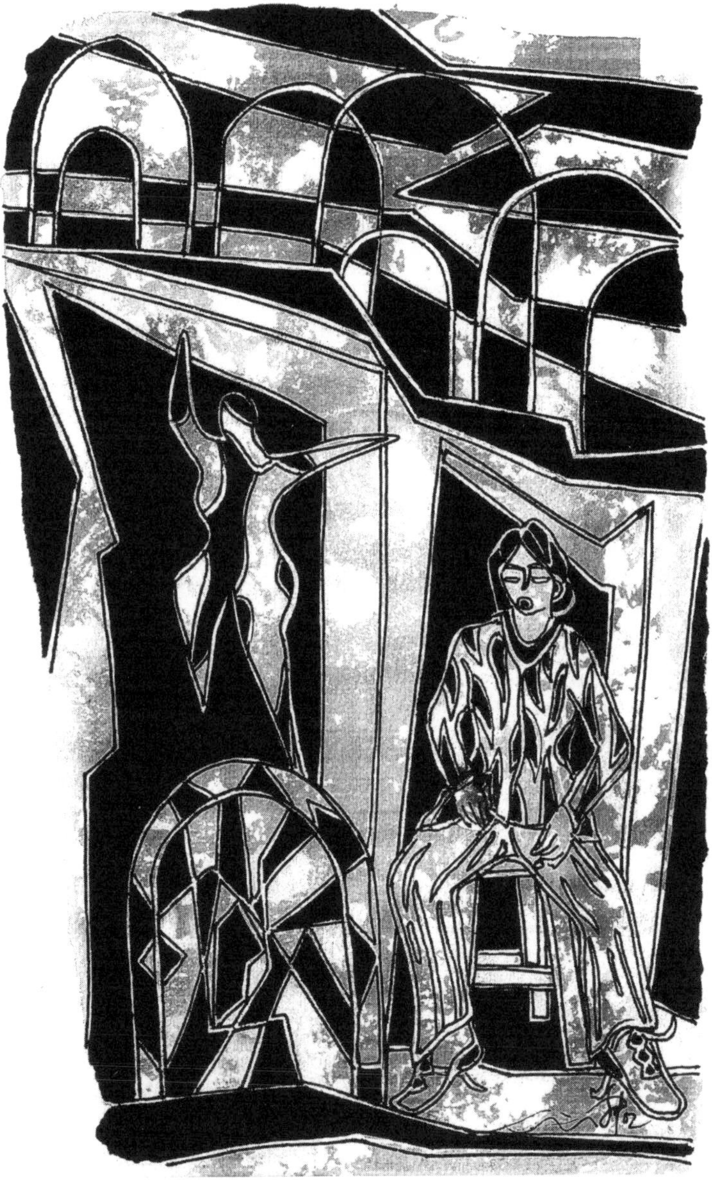

Plaza Río de Janeiro

A LONG TIME AGO, when I was a child and would only go see Mexican movies at the theatres in the seismic Andean city of Manizales, I forged an image of Mexico City linked to the buildings of the Roma neighborhood. Many years later, when I went to live in that city, I often walked through those streets that in face of the city's sweeping modernization survived like messages from a past full of glory and failure, poetry and death, monumentality and misery. I used to sit on a bench in the Plaza Río de Janeiro and contemplate the red brick castle located at the intersection of Durango and Orizaba in front of the old Colegio de México. Often, standing in front of the fountain of Michelangelo's David, I dreamt of living in that Witches' Castle constructed of chocolate and cardboard. A lot of my friends thought I was crazy: according to them, that would be the first building to collapse during some ominous earthquake.

Four years went by and chance and friendship led me to inhabit one of those apartments, the corner one where the afternoon sun would whistle through the windows. Through them I saw strange sleet and dreamy rain, high winds and dust storms, children playing with their mothers on the grass like in some legendary film, a thousand lovers kissing and touching each other behind the benches or next to the trees, the shouting of students and boy scouts, little girls dressed in blue uniforms and red cowls passing by daily. I heard, too, the sound of the *camote* vendors, a siren's nocturnal ululation, the dialogue of a couple taking refuge from the rain, the voices of friends.

The Mexico of those streets was the country I had dreamed about since childhood, for in the Colonia Roma I could feel myself at the turn of the century: the present epoch seems to me without greatness. Before the old red or gray brick buildings decorated with a nostalgic Parisian charm, the Roma took hold of me: drinking coffee in the legendary Bella Italia, buying the daily newspaper on a corner next to a church, visiting the bazaars, the antique shops, the rolling markets or the strange stores hidden inside a building that looked like a fantastic pastry.

In a short while I had become a child of the Colonia Roma, the Roma of today and yesterday that no longer exits, but which I then perceived within me and waking would dream of. The streets of Vasconcelos, Novo, Fuentes or Pacheco became more familiar to me than the distant ones of the Andean cities of Bogotá or Manizales. Living there through what seemed the most tragic decade in Mexican history, holding off the battles of a terrible crisis, I didn't know that in the depths of the earth, hiding inside subterranean caverns, the hidden gust of dreadful warriors prepared to whistle in the nocturnal north wind.

154

The 18th of September, 1985, I wrote until very late into the night. I felt some strange uneasiness, a fear that molded me to speak of hidden abysses where a warrior had fallen. I felt there the nefarious wind of geological concavities, the liquid killer magma of the rocks, the profound darkness of subterranean deserts covered with moss and stalactites and over the white page, mysteriously, I spoke of eyeless blackbirds beating their wings in the humid air of the eternal night. I felt something inside me, like a violet octopus. Strange forces came to announce something to me. Ravens touched my heart that night.

Seven hours later a terrible earthquake awoke me. I took my one-year-old daughter in my arms and followed by my wife went into the living room. The three of us stood beneath a door arch. We were shaking. Suddenly I felt the building sinking, falling over backward, dragging me toward the subterranean concavities. Then I saw a fissure forming like the rays of the devil and I heard the startling crack of the earth, the thundering sound of windows and live walls, the screech of electrical transformers accompanied by Luciferian sparks. At that moment, facing my wife and holding my one-year-old daughter in my arms, I thought everything was coming to an end. I try to open the door, but it's stuck between the walls. Impossible to open. In front of the apartment the distant street below. Impossible. We're going to die. Everything seems gray. Outside I can finally recall the silence of death. Everything stops. We manage to escape through the kitchen door and are the first to reach the Plaza Río de Janeiro.

In the text I wrote seven hours earlier, the man who falls into the subterranean abyss takes refuge in the plaza before Michelangelo's David, and alone there he sees arrive a stampede of sorrels that carry him to a distant continent situated near a mountain range. Perhaps nobody will believe what I say here. The pages lie before me and will become part of a novel. Literature can also be a premonition. Through it a nightmare had been revealed to me. The white horses that stopped to drink from the fountain of David were those which saved me and my friends, me and my family. The modern buildings in the vicinity collapsed or were destroyed; the Witches' Castle remained there unharmed, with some cracks, yes, but like a miraculous and absurd testimony to the past of Mexico. Like it, other red brick buildings constructed in 1910 or 1912 are still standing. The condominiums built with modern techniques fell.

Today I've come back to the devastated Roma. It's my Roma now. It not only belongs to Pacheco or Fuentes, or to the vampires. I was born in these streets I walk through. Obregón, Zacatecas, San Luis Potosí, Orizaba, Durango, Tabasco, Córdoba, Puebla. My streets. My Mexico. I can smell the odor of the corpses. I've seen the sidewalks in pieces, the solitude of the damned, I've been vaccinated against tetanus, although I know it doesn't matter. I've seen the solitary castle.

A frail eighty-year-old woman doesn't want to leave the building. "In 1939," she tells me, "my old man and I passed by here and this castle seemed beautiful to us. There were bellhops, an elevator, a fountain with goldfish. It was our first apartment and I've lived here for forty-five years; my children were born here." She goes to get water. I climb up the stairs. It's no longer the same: the tiles, the plants, the walls are sad; objects don't lie. I enter and go through the apart-

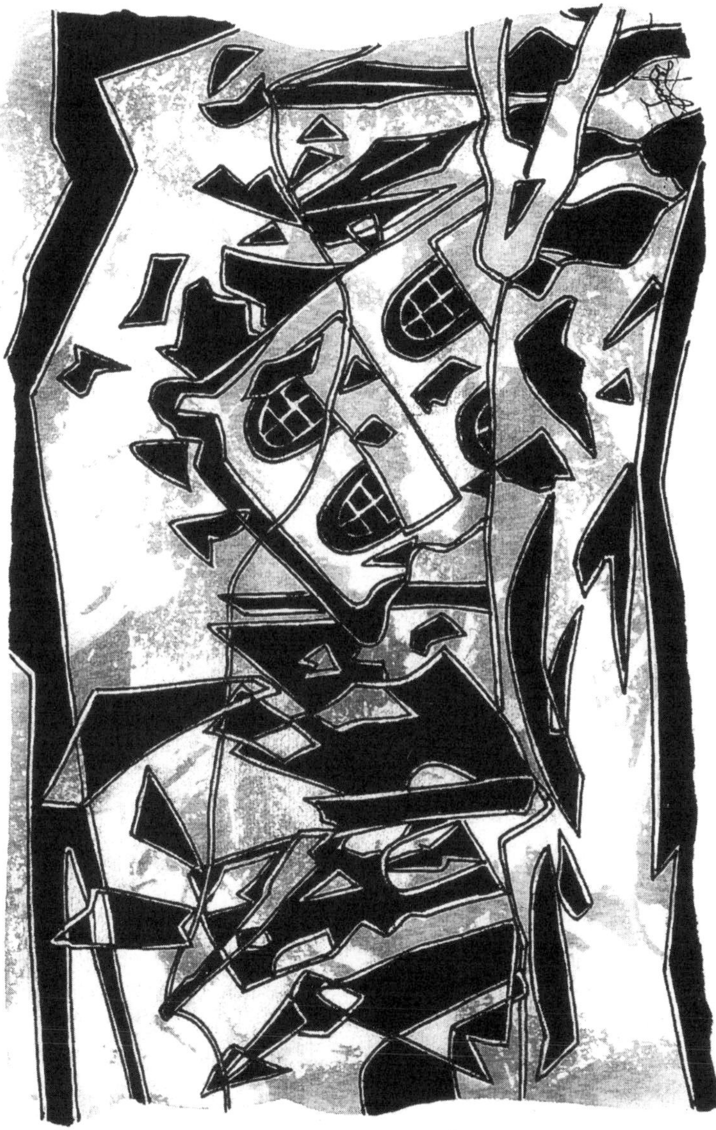

ment. It seems grayer than ever. I go to the studio that faces the corner of the park and wave at my friends from the window. Nothing no longer is or ever will be the same. This small idyll with the park has disappeared. Nurses slowly pass before the iliac David. A few old men with canes look at the other buildings, like the rectory that threatens to topple over. There are tents and cots, cars offering food and soft drinks. I go out with two suitcases and this green typewriter. I walk two blocks and take a taxi. I feel as if everything has changed. Neither this neighborhood nor myself will be the same. We are definitely exiled. The 19th of September those of us miraculously saved in the Colonia Roma are reborn. Which in a certain way is another kind of death.

Delirium in Coatzacoalcos

IN THE MIDDLE of an indomitable vegetation several beautiful oil wells painted light blue and yellow inexorably extract the black gold that gushes through the tubes like a whipping mass. The pulleys resound in the solitude, driving one tube that penetrates another. The apparatus seems to have its own life, like a giant long-beaked insect whose stinger drinks the earth's deep viscosity from a fountain. Beside it the only thing heard are the crickets chirping and in the depths of the landscape, above the vegetation, appears the mysterious smoke coming from the refineries, spreading out in the sky with neither end nor destiny.

Next to the enormous double piston of the well is an open puddle gurgling oil. A greasy greenish magma covers the nauseating liquid while several children play marbles next to their shack. For them the strange machine that has managed to spread through the vegetation is an animal like any other, perhaps an emanation of the earth itself. A woman hangs up the clothes she has just washed, a young man arrives on a bicycle and breaks through the jungle toward another hut where a few children await him. Soon a deep gurgling is heard and several bubbles break to the surface of the oily puddle and through the secret clefts of the tubes emerge little black streams that slowly slide by.

Everywhere there are rusty tubes covered by the vegetation, pieces of forgotten and useless machines, torn blackened gloves some worker long ago abandoned. The silence becomes more and more penetrating. From the top of a hill one sees here and there more wells spread out, according to the caprice of nature. Here one next to a tree, another hidden there amid the sylvan growth, that one over there in the ditch next to a highway leading nowhere. Amid the comforting green of the tropical zones, the blue color of the moving part of the mechanism, the yellow gold of the structure and the penetrating black of the crude oil all leap out. For a moment anyone might think the ancient deities had been replaced by these beings that suck sacrificial blood from the depths of the earth. Three iguanas suddenly emerge, pause for a moment and look at the inopportune visitor. Then they disappear, their steps resounding on the gravel. The wells aren't worried. Now and then sanguine men in hard hats approach their hinges, praying and imploring in muttering invocations. The visitor kneels and prays for several minutes and the sun burns his skin.

Not far from there the giant electrical towers seem even more impressive. Like prehistoric birds of which only the skeleton remains, they are united by cables shaken by the wind. Their truncated hands implore the heavens in a secret prayer known only to them and their creators. The visitor walks down a

161

beaten path and emerges onto a paved highway that loses itself from view in the vegetation. Passing by are cars, huge cargo vehicles, gas tankers, trailers stacked with pipes or automobiles. In the distance are the towers of the El Cangrejo Refinery, along with the enormous barrels from which the liquid emerges, completing an interminable process through the cooling towers and the sealed tubes that change the black gold into ethylene oxide, acetylene, polyethylene, benzene, toluene, orthoxylene, paraxylene, heavy aromatics, xylene mixtures, ethylbenzene, propane, butane, butilene, pentane, hexane, and naphtha.

On what was once the idyllic ranch of Don Amadeo Caballero there now extends a gigantic complex that roars and bellows with fury, expelling white vapors, infernal flames from which emerges a desperate black smoke that covers the tropical sky. Rectangular, cylindrical, conical, circular forms join together in a complex weave of iron ladders and bridges where from time to time men in overalls walk along only to be lost and devoured by the killer mouths of the vast machinery. Dense black blocks of towers and tubes watch over the sleeping soldiers. At a certain moment the workers begin emerging. Men with languid gazes and shining faces get in line next to a green bus. A few mixed blood and mulatto girls wait with their boyfriends next to the steps of an abandoned bridge. Those who once cut cane or hunted iguanas amid the crablike vegetation now take turns next to those tubes of the new civilization. The descendants of the Olmec civilization, lover of colossal deities, now adore the Tube God, the Omnipotent Oil Well, the Superior Council of Metallic Priests, the Goddess of the Refinery, the magic nectar coming from the magma, the

Sun God of progress. Those men who leave the complex have a disconcerted gaze and how could it be otherwise--they have passed hours, days, months, years amid a crush of men, and there no longer remains in them either the feeling or the idea of what the terrible delirium of Coatzacoalcos might be.

When you arrive to the bridge that crosses over a river the air turns heavy. The breeze mixing with ammonia smoke makes the ships invisible. Amid the absolute and poisoning invisibility, nevertheless, shines the spectacular orange sun that still cuts through the metallic cloak of air. A few rays spread a titillating path of languid red lines over the painted river. A sandy road leads the visitor through a desert landscape covered by bricks, rusty tubes, enormous obsolete installations and wrecked booths. A few people have installed themselves in brick houses there and on every block are a couple beer vendors who serve the thirsty pedestrians beneath the infernal sun. Little boys play soccer and little girls rock their rag dolls. Men repair big broken down American automobiles. Women sweep the doorways and throw water to squelch the dust.

The visitor continues on until he arrives to a filthy moribund beach that serves as a dump for rusty car bodies. The road borders the sea and in the distance lies the line of enormous cargo ships, unimaginable cisterns that sleepily await their turn to load the black gold. There are five, ten, perhaps fifteen embarcations sketching their superstructures upon the horizon. He passes through new neighborhoods with bars whose jukebox love songs crash against the walls and abandoned puddles. New truncated avenues are glimpsed in their solitude on every side, and suddenly

163

he sees some factory that went into bankruptcy, leaving strange tubes behind to the elements, and then the river upon which little boats sail.

On the other side of Wharf #9 are the refineries and port installations. With binoculars one can see the noisy longshoremen, the ant-like movement of certain officials and soldiers with rifles, the solitude of a white lighthouse whose mythic function is the only thing that brightens this desert of sand and iron. The visitor sees the ships waiting for something known to no one. One is called "Birdie" and another "The Gulf Stream." The water crashes against their black hulls and their superstructures, empty and unprovisioned from the voyage's latest activity, seem interplanetary ships forgotten in a corner of some forgotten world. They are ships from the end of the world. A few capricious birds fly over the lunar landscape of progress. With a certain cynicism they give a real touch to a zone already anchored in the future and whose past is an impossible nostalgia. What was once the lost paradise is today the realm of ineluctable disaster. The visitor knows that and for this reason takes photographs with his fiery eyes. He looks at the late afternoon and scratches his hoofs, his horns and his tail. He lifts his satanic trident and his shadow turns the refuse of time to ashes.

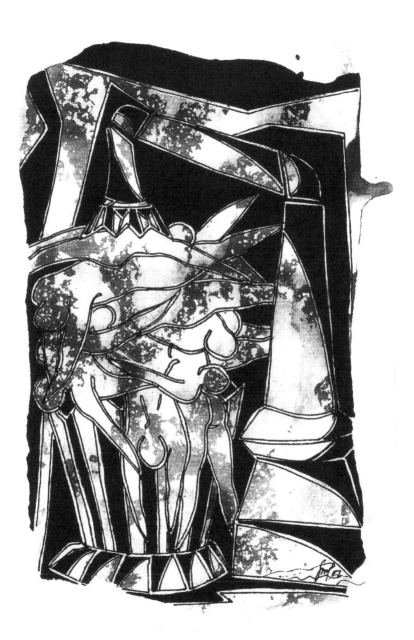

Chronicle of the Luminous City

FROM THE LATIN AMERICAN Tower's twenty-eighth floor the vision of the metropolis is quite fantastic. As the months go by, each afternoon or dawn takes on new contortions and the rain or the dust, the humidity or the dryness, the whistling wind or the inclement sun offer us in their guises an unknown and mysterious city. Down below when you run from one place to another amid the inhuman agitation, the city becomes an incomprehensible inferno and the grind is blinding. From up on high, on the contrary, the urb can become a silent friend and accomplice. Most beautiful are the afternoons. The sun falls obliquely over the extensive lost neighborhoods and from the depths of Texcoco project rainbows that break the fury of the dusty whirlwinds. On some clear days, to the south seem to slowly disappear the enigmatic mountains and volcanoes whose knowledge is only attained after wandering a long time in these lands. To the north the hills, already eaten away by new neighborhoods, erupt with splendor and devour human enterprise. Later

167

night falls. Neon lights sketch long astonishing unending serpentine avenues and a weave of little lights covers what was a short while ago a flat and stalking beast. Airplanes land and at ground level, almost atop the roofs, they hit the runway and it all appears as if you were right there. On a nearby mountain a bright light emits intermittent signals. Soon a bolt of lightning cracks the night and the storm begins. The urb, finally tamed, lets the wind run through it, crashing now against the windows of the Tower, provoking a macabre whistle. Luminous flashes of lightening course through the skies. Black clouds overpower the night and a rainstorm pours through the windows. A ballad of water. Galactic humidity. A sensation of peace strengthens the nocturnal spectator. Someone thinks this entire mass of buildings might disintegrate during the night and at daybreak a fertile land replace the metropolis.

But that's not what happens. At six in the morning the city is there, unharmed. Little clouds of smoke surge from certain buildings, hotels perhaps, and Mexico City seems like the engraving of a Renaissance painter. Activity is just beginning. A few helicopters cross the skies, pointing out to drivers which routes are jammed, where the one-ways and the impossible intersections are. At times the volcanoes clearly appear in the light coming from their distant side. The splendor of the new day reveals church cupolas and the palaces that for centuries made the city famous throughout the world. From this height the observer transposes himself to idyllic epochs and sees Bolívar and Humboldt walking through the streets, or he crosses a park and sees priests recruiting more faithful to their liturgy. Over there the Plaza de Santo

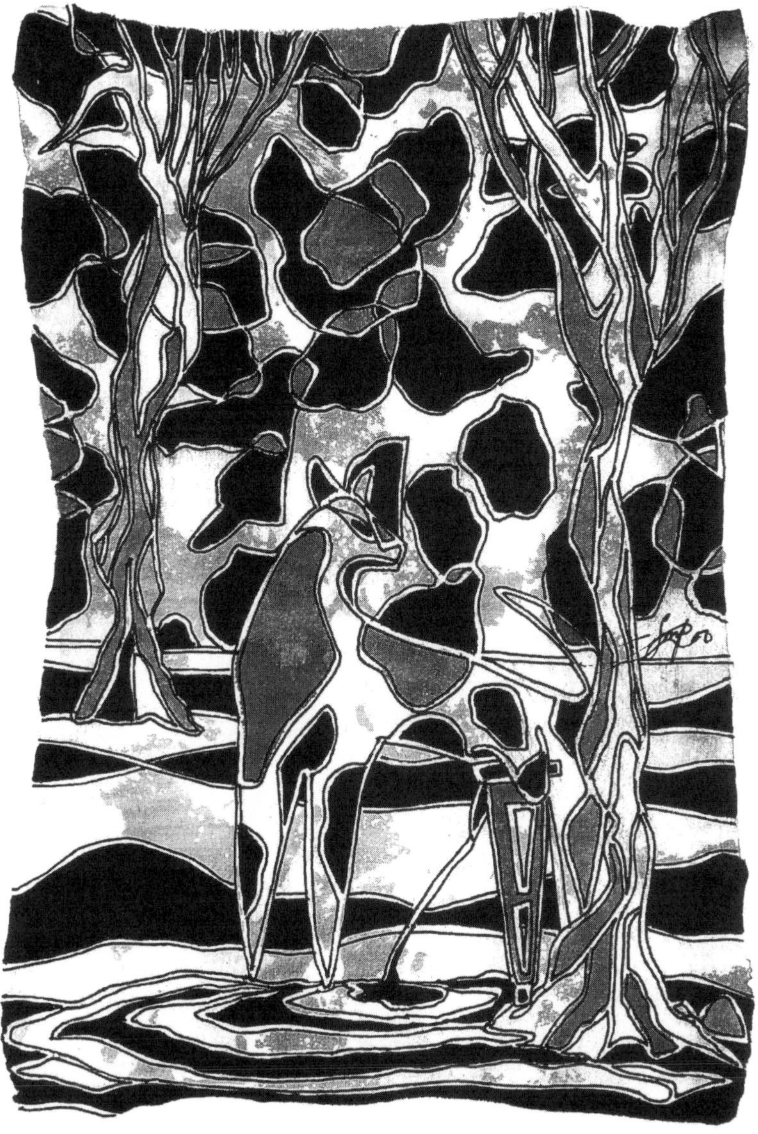

Domingo, the customs building, over here the Palace of Iturbide, there the Metropolitan Cathedral, and farther still the Avenue of the Mysteries, canals, cultivated fields, churches, Chapultepec Park. A diminutive little city full of baroque and rococo altars inundated with incense. In that downtown of cheap hotels and splendid houses walked the young Vasconcelos, in old workshops were printed newspapers and magazines, in cafés now vanished were hatched riots and revolutions. The modernist poets edited their marvelous heliotropic verses here. The young ministers of Huerta and the writers who—like González Martínez, Tablada and López Portillo—assisted him, used to hold conversation here, before the revolutionaries came. In variety theatres are still heard the *cuples* and the *tandas* of an agonizing Porfirianism. Maximiliano, disguised as an Indian, hides behind an arcade. The blond woman Rodríguez is kissed by a young government official. A nun flees with a vagabond toward Tlalpan. In the Alameda crackles the flesh of an unredeemed Jew and the burning smell reaches us. A hundred bodies burn next to the Ciudadela. A nostalgic Amado Nervo walks down Moneda Street.

A sudden blaze of fire appears, nevertheless, from the other side of the city: the smoky clouds and burning flames of the Azcapotzalco refinery. The dream has ended, sirs, and the observer can't believe his eyes. The long flames, menacing and luxurious, spread out in a vast expanse: the devil has come out with his own fire. The savage bellowing of a smokestack accompanies the undulating figures of black and white smoke. Those that appear look like the snouts of monstrous basilisks, fire-eating dragons. The insupportable blanket of fog gathers strength above the

171

city until midday and by one o'clock a terrible suffocation forces us to drink liters of water. The spectator's face is covered by grease. The intersection at Lázaro Cárdenas Avenue is a demonic anthill. The horns of a thousand vehicles and the sirens of ambulances resound. The dust of buildings being demolished takes the breath away from passers-by. A crazy woman who's always hanging around the Palace of Fine Arts can be seen from up here proffering her incomprehensible insults. A new crazy woman who for several days has blown a whistle like a referee on the corner near the post office is there, too, and with a pair of binoculars the spectator watches her raise her hand to warn of catastrophe. A painter arrives to the Palace of Fine Arts with an enormous canvas. In the Alameda a rock band contributes to the dementia's rising decibel level. A woman is run over by an ambulance. A one-eyed dog pisses on a dying tree.

By three-thirty in the afternoon a metallic plate covers the entire city. The mountains have disappeared. A building collapses on a fat old lady selling lottery tickets. The cortege of a big politician heads for the Zócalo down Madero Street. The same dog that not long ago was pissing on a dying tree has been hit by a bus. A dirty old pigeon crashes against the window on the twenty-eighth floor and its blood sketches the abstract and arcane figure of a virgin. People go from one place to another and out of little holes workers leave and enter, having just finished ingesting a scant meal that cost them a fortune. The child selling gum, the blind men singing sad songs in a passage on Tacuba Street, sweaty organ players rushing upon the city-dwellers whose gaze is more lost than hopeful. The metallic plate continues descending and suddenly the city disappears from the observer's sight. The drone of turbines sounds. The windows of the Latin American Tower shake. The walls crackle. The building starts to tilt a bit and then starts to rise into the heavens, having turned into a rocket. The observer, who loves this city with an indestructible passion, straps on a parachute and jumps into the purulent void. Coughing in the smog, he returns to his adored streets and then disappears into the confusion of the afternoon crowd.

Caribbean Express

IN RIOHACHA, capital of Guajira, the farthest Caribbean corner in continental Colombia, they only listen to the *vallenato*. It's a catchy, rhythmic music that accompanies sad lyrics, complete histories that form the saga of coastal customs. In neighborhoods of dirt streets, the Guajiros drink Cristal *aguardiente* and beer in the back gardens of houses and the girls, barefoot and wearing diaphanous dresses, dance to the rhythm of Binomio de Oro, the vallenato duo that's all the craze. "Burn her up! Burn her up!" goes one song while the Caribbean breeze blows down the streets.

On the border with Venezuela, Guajira is a lawless land. Throughout the length and width of the state cars have Venezuelan license plates instead of Colombian ones. Enormous American automobiles costing a couple thousand dollars at the most drive down the bare streets. In little stores on street corners or at stalls one finds every kind of liquor at ridiculous prices. The best French champagne at seven dollars a bottle, Rémy Martin for six, the most exquisite whiskeys for five, the best wines from Rioja for four. In the streets vendors give away French soaps and perfumes. In Maicao, the paradise of smuggled Caribbean goods, entire streets are filled with exotic products from all over the world, merchandise that ships have left behind in their wake. A center for drug traffickers as well, Guajira has seen billions of dollars pass through its streets that still remain sad and bare.

Legend has it that the Guajiros will kill for any reason at all. On the same corner of Riohacha, young black men invite in the *cachaco*s, those from Bogotá, and tell them incredible stories: entire families decimated for a girl's "honor," like in *Chronicle of a Death Foretold*.

"They killed my cousin yesterday at a fiesta, that's why I don't want my sister dancing in the street," says a drunken Guajiro, carrying a bottle of *aguardiente* in his hand.

The next day, in the central square where at the only movie theatre García Márquez's *Time to Die* has been playing for the last week, a daughter of the local nobility marries a magistrate's son. Beneath the 100-degree dog day sun, politicians and government officials dressed like *cachacos* arrive in their neckties and starched-collared shirts. While the walls melt in the heat, old women sitting at the front of the church dressed in black dresses and Spanish shawls, like Ursula Iguarán, don't even sweat. Mass begins. A few blocks farther on is the wharf García Márquez immortalized in *Love in the Time of Cholera*, the palm trees and the customs house the eyes of Fermina Daza saw when she was forced into exile from Riohacha. Her father sent her here, to this end of the earth, to prevent her from marrying Florentino Ariza.

Not a sole tourist is on the beach. This *cachaco* can brag about being the only one here this week. You can walk a hundred meters into the surf without worrying about being dragged under by the waves. And next to a ten-story building that was once supposed to be a hotel but now looks like a dinosaur skeleton is seen a million varieties of sea shells, strewn along by the surf. Next to the wharf old fishing boats surviving from the Second World War slowly rock in a shipwrecked and nostalgic past. The building, which could have been the seed of tourism for the city, was never completed because its owner was cut down in a hale of bullets for business reasons.

In the middle of the city is an air-conditioned library where one finds all kinds of books. From every corner of this exotic country come school children and university language professors to read Octavio Paz. Incredible but true, such is the devotion of young people in Colombia for the Mexican writer that in this lost city at the ends of the earth not only can one buy Moët Chandon and Rémy Martin, but as well *The Bow and the Lyre* and *Children of the Mire*. In the plaza the affluence of the *cachacos* from Antioquia is boundless. They are the best merchants and have a monopoly on stores and cafés. Some say those from the coast live more happily in Bogotá than on the seashore and no one looks happier than a *cachaco* in the Caribbean.

Leaving Riohacha one sees the snowy mountaintop of Santa Marta, a piece of cold earth next to the sea, a snowy peak that can be seen from the beach. On air-conditioned buses equipped with closed-circuit television one can travel along the coast in complete comfort. In the distance lies Santa Marta, beside

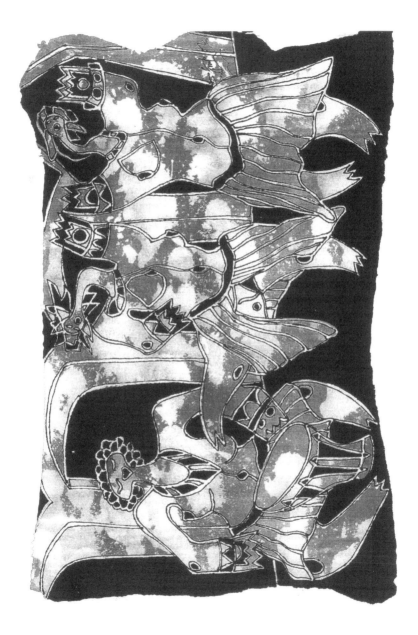

the road rest turn-of-the-century mansions destroyed by salt and an unending swamp filled with dead tree branches. There died General Simon Bolívar at the country house of San Pedro Alejandrino, and they say many of the best members of the group M-19 come from this white city. The impeccable highway leads us through interminable swamps. The snowy peak appears in the distance and we manage to discern the roads that carried Fermina Márquez on her exile from Riohacha through the little villages where, with the complicity of the telegraph operators, the young woman received messages from her anachronistic and quasi-*cachaco* lover.

Attention: the mouth of the Magdalena River. Immense, reddened by mud, the river extends with all its charging force and breaks through to the ocean. It comes from southern Colombia and has crossed the entire country in order to deposit its sap on these 98-degree coasts and its insupportable stupor that kills people at midday during those iguana siestas. And like an absurd vision or an emanation of dementia appears Barranquilla, the metallic city of skyscrapers and unending neighborhoods growing in the mist beneath the fiery sun. From the bus one sees the blinding gleams projected by the tin roofs and glass windows of the buildings. In the streets boys play soccer or imitate the world boxing champion "Happy" Lora, the nation's new idol.

Barranquilla is the coastal metropolis, a commercial center where the most important newspapers are published and whose vigorous cultural tradition has inaugurated in its time Ramón Vinyes, the "wise Catalan" of *One Hundred Years of Solitude*, and Álvaro Cepeda Samudio, the founder of modern journalism in Colombia. In this city of the cold earth built beside the Caribbean flourished the Grupo de Barranquilla, from which emerged Gabriel García Márquez.

Cartagena, on the contrary, survives only by its beauty. Still intact are the ramparts that withstood the attacks of English pirates and protected the immense riches coming from the south and the north that were weighed here before leaving for Spain. A few kilometers away was found the galleon San José along with its invaluable riches, scattered along the bottom of the sea. In *Love in the Time of Cholera* some rogue tricks Florentino into believing that he is on the point of recovering the jewels and buried gold. Cartagena is a protagonist in this novel and one can pass through the market where Fermina understood that Florentino was just some poor devil, visit the neighborhood of Manga where Juvenal and Fermina lived happily, and see a house identical to the one where the doctor died trying to get the parrot down from the tree.

The downtown is as it was two hundred, three hundred years ago. The wide balconies providing shade, the landings, the patios, the cisterns, the long porches, the corridors full of the ghosts of inquisitors, renegades and converts. The Palace of the Inquisition, the church of Santo Domingo, the temple of the Jesuits, the bay of souls. At night one sees Blas de Lezo, the limping one-eyed, one-armed man who defended the city against a pirate ship and is today the mythological hero of the city. The cannons are still in line ready to fire at the enemy, and in the house of the Marquis of Valdehoyos, who in García Márquez's novel is named Casalduero, are seen two enormous beautifully colored papagayos, solitary parrots in the middle of the unforgettable Cartagena night, looking at you from centuries past.

During the day, when Cartagena awakes and one sees its citizens walking in the narrow allies or going into the old taverns, there is light, and then you realize not only is this the Caribbean's most beautiful and preserved city, but all those who journey here to experience it enter into an inscrutable dimension of fantasy.

A Note on the Author, the Illustrator, and the Translator

Eduardo García Aguilar was born in the Andean city of Manizales, Colombia, in 1953. After being graduated in political economy from the University of Paris, he moved to Mexico City where he wrote for a number of newspapers and magazines, eventually becoming assistant director of Agence France-Presse. In the late 1990s he returned to Paris, where he currently heads the Latin American desk for AFP and is a frequent contributor to *Letras Libres*. But more than being a journalist, García Aguilar has had a prolific literary career, having written two collections of short stories, two collections of poetry, and three novels, including *El Viaje Triunfal,* winner of the 1993 Premio Ernesto Sábato. He has also published book-length studies of his compatriots Álvaro Mutis and Gabriel García Márquez.

A native of Bogotá, Colombia, Santiago Rebolledo Arango studied painting, drawing, and printmaking before coming to Mexico in 1975. He has shown his work in venues such as the Museo Rufino Tamayo, the Museo de Arte Carrillo Gil, and the Instituto Nacional de Bellas Artes in Mexico City, as well as galleries throughout Latin America and Europe.

Rebolledo, who has also taught painting and lithography, was co-founder of the artists collective Grupo SUMA and a member of the Foro de Arte Contemporáneo in Mexico. He currently lives in Oaxaca.

Jay Miskowiec received his Ph.D. in comparative literature from the City University of New York, where he studied with Gregory Rabassa. He has translated two other books by Eduardo García Aguilar, the novel *Boulevard of Heroes* and his examination of globalism and Latin America, *Mexico Madness: Manifesto for a Disenchanted Generation.* His translations from the French include Michel Foucault's "Of Other Spaces" and Simone de Beauvoir's "Toward a Morals of Ambiguity, According to Pyrrhus and Cinéas."

Miskowiec is the translation editor of Aliform Publishing and curator of its online gallery.